THE COMPLETE PEGAN DIET FOR BEGINNERS

THE COMPLETE

PEGAN DIET *for*

BEGINNERS

A **14-DAY WEIGHT LOSS MEAL PLAN** *with* **OVER 50 EASY RECIPES**

AMELIA LEVIN

Photography by Marija Vidal

ROCKRIDGE
PRESS

For general information on our other products and services or to obtain technical support, please contact our Customer Care Department within the United States at (866) 744-2665, or outside the United States at (510) 253-0500.

Rockridge Press publishes its books in a variety of electronic and print formats. Some content that appears in print may not be available in electronic books, and vice versa.

TRADEMARKS: Rockridge Press and the Rockridge logo are trademarks or registered trademarks of Callisto Media Inc. and/or its affiliates, in the United States and other countries, and may not be used without written permission. All other trademarks are the property of their respective owners. Rockridge Press is not associated with any product or vendor mentioned in this book.

Interior and Cover Designer: Lisa Forde
Art Producer: Janice Ackerman
Editor: Pam Kingsley
Production Editor: Andrew Yackira
Author photo courtesy of Bauwerks Photography Studio (Chicago).

Cover Photography: © 2019 Marija Vidal. Food styled by Elisabet der Nederlanden.

Interior Photography by: © 2019 Darren Muir: Title Page, Introduction, p. 14, 22, 38, 52, 66.

Contents Page: © Helene Dujardin

P. 2., P. 104. © Nadine Greeff

P. 38. © Cameron Whitman / Stocksy

P. 116. © GoncharukMaks / Shutterstock

ISBN: Print 978-1-64152-678-4 | eBook 978-1-64152-679-1

Dedicated to Harvey Henao: my husband, the best Daddy ever, my No. 1 taste-tester for this book and others, and my "rock" in life. I also dedicate this book to our taste-testers-in-training, Jonah and Liliana (Lily).

Berry Power Smoothie, page 41

CONTENTS

INTRODUCTION

Allow me to explain my introduction to the Paleo world, which ultimately led me into Pegan territory.

Nearly a decade ago, I joined a CrossFit® gym with my now-husband as a way to stay active, shed a few pounds, and strengthen my ankle, which had been injured from too many long-distance runs. The workouts were incredibly challenging, even for someone—like me—who thought she was already in great shape. But we loved Cross-Fit and how strong it made us feel, both mentally and physically.

The admittedly cultlike culture of CrossFit strongly encourages its participants to adopt a Paleo diet, which excludes all grains, dairy, sugar, and processed foods. The diet includes foods in their natural form, such as fresh vegetables, berries, grass-fed meat, eggs from free-range poultry, avocados, nuts, seeds, and certain unrefined, minimally processed oils to build energy and lean muscle mass while maximizing performance at the gym.

The idea behind the Paleo diet is that you can support your body and improve your health if you eat the way our Paleolithic ancestors did before agriculture—a time when people would hunt for wild animals and feast on nuts, berries, and plants. Well, I liked the sound of that, so I tried it.

After just one week of following the Paleo diet, the results were astounding. I began to have more energy—physically and mentally. After the first month, that energy became boundless. The brain fog I didn't realize I had for so long cleared up, and my anxiety calmed down. I wrote cookbooks such as *Paleo for Every Day: 4 Weeks of Paleo Diet Recipes & Meal Plans to Lose Weight & Improve Health* and countless magazine articles. I didn't even have to get on a scale to know I was losing weight; I could feel it. More importantly, my body became resculpted, and for the better. I started to notice curves in my biceps. My stomach started shrinking little by little, and my legs grew stronger by the day.

These results were not only due to my workouts; they also had to do with the food I was choosing to put—or not put—in my mouth. The way I was eating would ultimately support the kind of fat loss and muscle growth I craved. About a year after going Paleo, however, I began to question the amount of meat allowed on the Paleo diet. While my husband enjoys meat at most meals, and that works for him, I noticed that I felt a little less sluggish if I skipped meat from time to time. I was also becoming concerned about the ethical issues of consuming meat regularly, especially if it wasn't pasture-raised, and even if it was labeled organic or antibiotic- and hormone-free.

VEGAN + PALEO = PEGAN

For nine years, the Paleo and Pegan diets, or some combination thereof, have helped me get through two bad waves of postpartum depression, fit back into my skinny jeans, and supply me with the mental energy and physical stamina that two kids under the age of five and a full-time career demand.

Over time, however, it became hard to define my evolving diet. I knew I had more energy if I balanced my meals with meat and more plant-based foods. I wasn't exactly a vegan, because I enjoyed eggs every day. I wasn't a pescatarian or vegetarian, because I ate the occasional chicken or steak. I'm also not a huge fan of grains, not because Paleo purists eschew them, but because it's time-consuming to cook big batches of quinoa or amaranth on a regular basis. Beans? Well, let's just say that they make me feel a little bloated, and, ahem, they have some other not-so-nice effects as well. Still, I have always liked the occasional lentil soup or homemade hummus. And, although I have had some success on the Keto diet, which permits dairy, I didn't love the idea of adopting it on a long-term basis due to my lactose sensitivity. Plus, Keto just felt a little restrictive.

At this point, I wondered, what diet was I following?

I decided to stop trying to pigeonhole my diet and just focus on the foods that I know make me feel great. Then I came across Dr. Mark Hyman.

Dr. Hyman, the medical director at the Cleveland Clinic's Center for Functional Medicine, originated the idea of eating more plant-based meals without missing out on the healthy protein, vitamin B_{12}, and high iron counts that only meat and fish can provide. Dr. Hyman said the word Pegan one day when he was on a panel, seated in between a vegan and a Paleo eater, and mentioned that he felt like he had a lot in common with both sides. "I guess I'm a Pegan!" he exclaimed. The term clearly stuck with me, and I finally had a name for the diet that worked for me.

Though vegan and Paleo might seem like polar opposites on paper, when combined, they offer a much more balanced diet in both nutrition and flavor. I like to think of Pegan as the best of both worlds. It's a diet rich in fresh, clean, delicious, and natural foods such as colorful vegetables, low-sugar fruit, healthy protein, and good fats, while eliminating processed foods, added sugars, hormone-ridden dairy, bread, pasta, and grains, all of which can lead to chronic inflammation in the body. Following a Pegan lifestyle, Dr. Hyman tells us, can help us ward off diabetes, heart disease, and even autoimmune conditions, especially as we age. I personally experienced clearer skin and reduced anxiety, and shed a few pounds along the way.

There's another awesome benefit of going Pegan. Eating more plant-based meals not only fuels us with all the vitamins and minerals we need to stay healthy and ward off disease, we're doing our part to reduce our carbon footprint by saying no to commercial meat production. When we choose not to eat meat from animals that were shoved together in confined spaces and feedlots, pumped full of antibiotics, and fed genetically modified organism (GMO)– and pesticide-laced soy and corn, we're doing right by the animals and by ourselves.

Although the word "diet" is in the title of this book, I like to think of Pegan as a true lifestyle shift. In addition to eating the best possible foods you can eat for optimal health, the Pegan lifestyle can have a positive impact on emotions around food and on mental clarity and focus. Most importantly, it can make you feel great. Stick with it, and the benefits will only increase over time.

Don't worry about people thinking you're a granola-loving vegan or a voracious carnivore. Forget about labeling yourself this or that. Just say hello to the new, healthier you.

How Can This Diet Be Vegan If It Includes Meat?

Even though the term Pegan is derived from the word vegan, don't be fooled. There's a reason Dr. Hyman does not recommend a diet that eliminates meat, fish, and eggs. Vegans can struggle to get adequate levels of iron and protein. According to Dr. Hyman, these nutrients are especially important as the body ages and loses muscle mass. In addition, vitamin B_{12} is only found naturally in meat; it's added to commercial bread products and cereals. Vegans who skip these products, however, need to take supplements, which can be inadequate.

Instead of putting the kibosh on any kind of meat or fish, the Pegan diet allows for selective choices when you do decide to eat meat. The omega-3 fatty acids found in sustainably sourced fish and in pasture-raised meat and eggs far surpass those found in commercially raised animals and cage-free eggs from grain-fed chickens. It's all about choosing wisely, reading labels, and knowing where your food comes from.

HOW TO USE THIS BOOK

Part 1 of this book contains the guidelines and benefits of the Pegan diet. It will explain why you should eat some foods and not others. It will also provide you with a 14-day Pegan Jumpstart Plan as well as a list of Pegan-friendly foods to ignite this way of eating. This section also contains advice on how to maintain your Pegan lifestyle after completing the Jumpstart Plan.

Part 2 offers 50 delicious recipes to start you on the road to sustained weight loss as well as overall good health, so that you can continue to enjoy the benefits of the Pegan diet.

The best thing about this 14-day Jumpstart Plan is that it allows you to begin your journey toward a better you. It works well even if you already have a fairly healthy diet, yet you want to try something new. You can return to the 14-day plan if you ever stray from the Pegan diet and want to shed a few pounds.

Note that you don't have to follow the Pegan diet to a T, either. Feel free to swap breakfast, lunch, or dinner suggestions throughout each day. Feel like eggs at dinner? Go for it! Hankering for a little meat in the middle of the day? Eat it! Though I work mostly at home, I do go into an office a couple days a week and, as mentioned, have young children, so I like to take the weekends to make batches of food like Paleo granola, meatballs, bone broth, and some sweet treats so that I have a few things ready to go during the week. That way I won't fall prey to salt- (and sometimes sugar-) laden, expensive delivery foods or poor-quality convenience foods.

Another important thing to note: While there are many Pegan-friendly ingredients on the market, such as nut flours, nut milks, and other pantry staples, this book is meant for beginners on the diet. You should be able to find the ingredients for all of these recipes at your regular grocery store or supermarket or, as a last resort, at a specialty grocer or online.

PART I

THE PEGAN DIET

Eating the Pegan way is nothing new, really. Think of it as travelling back in time, before we worried about pesticides in our veggies and microwaved meals came in cardboard boxes. Pegan is not a trend, nor is it a fad, nor even a true diet. It's a shift to a whole new lifestyle, one that will help you become the best you that you ever imagined.

I'll start slowly. Chapter 1 will cover the tenets of the Pegan lifestyle and diet. Chapter 2 will get into the many health benefits of the diet and help you with the basics of the Pegan pantry. By chapter 3, you'll be ready to get into the 14-day Pegan Jumpstart Plan.

Pegan Diet Basics

The Pegan diet is all about fresh, wholesome foods, enjoyed in balance with each other and in accordance with what your body naturally craves. Nutritionists always say to eat the rainbow by loading up on fresh vegetables and fruits, and that is sound advice. When you adopt a Pegan mentality, you'll be able to determine what works best for you.

EATING THE PEGAN WAY

The Pegan way of eating is about making better selections when it comes to the foods you choose to eat, want to eat less of, or not eat at all. These choices not only have a direct impact on your health and spirit, but they also impact our environment.

EAT PLANTS (WITH A SIDE OF ANIMAL PROTEIN)

Plants—and a wide variety at that—provide us with boundless energy and the vitamins and minerals we need to fuel our days. The Pegan diet encourages us to make meals comprised of 75 percent fresh and, ideally, pesticide-free produce. This suggestion is also a 100 percent disrupter of how many describe the standard American diet.

A 4- to 6-ounce portion of meat or fish works best, providing us with important vitamins and minerals, such as B_{12}, iron, potassium, zinc, and phosphorus, that are difficult or impossible to get from an exclusively vegan diet. Grass-fed meat also contains conjugated linoleic acids, which help with fat loss, lean muscle development, and diabetes prevention. These acids even have antioxidants such as beta carotene and vitamin K. Sustainably produced meat, fish, and eggs also have a smaller carbon footprint, putting less pressure on the environment as a whole.

Depending on where you live, it's also beneficial to eat a more plant-based diet using seasonal ingredients. There is a reason why we crave bright green vegetables after a long, cold winter; lighter, sweeter vegetables in the summer when the mercury rises; and heartier produce as the weather cools in autumn, especially as we're craving more sustenance to sustain the "hibernating" to come. Our bodies are telling us what we need, and when.

So, in short, eating a diet consisting mainly of plants—with some meat, fish and omega-3 rich eggs—ensures you'll get all the nutrients, including protein, you need to not just function, but live, and live well.

EAT GOOD FATS

If you grew up in the fat-phobic eighties and nineties, you're likely familiar with the host of processed foods loudly labeled "low-fat" and "fat-free" during that time. These types of foods still exist today. Thank goodness we now know that the perception these foods are healthy is bonkers. These heavily processed foods not only substitute salt and sugar for the missing flavor that real, healthy fat provides, they also carry all sorts of other additives.

In his books, Dr. Hyman cites studies that show processed foods, consumed over time, can cause increased consumption of omega-6 fatty acids, mainly in the form of highly refined safflower, sunflower, and canola oils, and—worse—trans fats in the form of margarine. A diet high in these omega-6 fatty acids and low in healthy omega-3s can lead to chronic inflammation and the development of small holes in the intestinal lining, allowing toxins to enter the bloodstream. Omega-3 rich fatty acids in the form of whole foods such as sustainably sourced fish, avocados, nuts of all kinds, as well as pasture-raised eggs and grass-fed butters can do wonders for your health, not to mention your skin and overall mental well-being.

Dr. Hyman, in his book *Food: What The Heck Should I Eat?*, points out that once-demonized saturated fat, particularly fat sourced from grass-fed and sustainably raised animals, actually has no negative impact on heart health or cholesterol levels. In fact, quality saturated fats can actually raise healthy cholesterol levels (HDLs). And while dairy from cow's milk should be minimized on the Pegan diet, grass-fed butter is allowed as it's rich in omega-3 fatty acids. If you have a lactose intolerance, you can make your own clarified butter by straining out the whey for a healthy fat with a high smoke point. (See the Meat-Free Eggs Benedict with Lemon Hollandaise Sauce on page 48.)

Healthy fat, in addition to fueling our brains and bodies, has another important benefit: it assists with the absorption of fat-soluble vitamins such as A and K. So don't be afraid to drizzle a little extra-virgin olive oil over your vegetables or eat an avocado or nuts with just about anything. Your food will taste better and be better for you.

LESSEN THE SUGAR LOAD

I'm not going to sugarcoat this. Sugar is really, really harmful. Many people are addicted to it and don't even know it, and that included me several years ago. Cutting out sugar has helped me control my once-dramatic cravings, binge-eating tendencies, low energy levels, and weight. It has also done wonders for my skin.

Sugar comes in sneaky forms such as flavored yogurt, even nondairy yogurt, as well as chicken sausage, bacon, and many nutrition bars. As such, it is important to check labels carefully and always remain on the lookout for sugars and sweeteners, including the artificial kind.

Glycemic Index/Glycemic Load

The glycemic index (GI) was created by two doctors at the University of Toronto. It measures how quickly foods containing carbohydrates raise blood glucose levels and ranks them on a scale of 0 to 100. Researchers at Harvard later developed the glycemic load (GL) to measure digestible carbohydrates and their impact on blood glucose levels over the course of a meal or entire day. Glycemic load also takes fiber, serving size, and cooking method into account.

Glycemic load is calculated by multiplying the grams of a food's carbohydrates by its glycemic index number, and then dividing by 100. For example, watermelon has a high GI, but one serving does not contain as many carbohydrates as bread, so the glycemic load is low. Carbohydrates with a low GI value (55 or less) are digested, absorbed, and metabolized more slowly, and result in smaller blood glucose and insulin level increases, which would otherwise stimulate fat storage.

Although GI and GL were developed to treat those with type 2 diabetes, anyone can benefit from restricting foods with a higher glycemic index. Studies show that low, stabilized blood sugar levels can have many benefits, including sustained weight loss and less abdominal fat..

A glycemic index of 55 or less is considered low, 56 to 69 is moderate, and 70 and above is high. A glycemic load of 10 or less is low, 11 to 19 is moderate, and 20 or more is high.

You may have heard more about clean eating lately. This means focusing on eating foods in their whole form, such as fruits, vegetables, and quality proteins and fats versus processed foods, packaged foods, refined oils, and even some dairy products. Eating clean not only has a positive impact on our physical and mental health, it also helps the environment. When we minimize ingestion of foods that contain antibiotics, pesticides, GMOs, hormones, mercury, and additives, and choose organic foods and foods that have been humanely raised or sustainably farmed or harvested, we're creating less demand for commercial agriculture and meat and greater demand for a safer, more Earth-friendly food supply.

Buying Organic

The "USDA certified" organic certification ensures that produce was grown under certain conditions and without the use of chemical-based fertilizers or pesticides. Increasingly, general grocery markets are expanding their organic produce sections, making these foods more available and affordable than they have ever been. You can also find organic foods at your local farmers' market, though they may not have the certified organic label, perhaps due to the costly and bureaucratic certification process.

If organic produce is out of your price range, certain fruits and vegetables with thicker skins or peels such as avocados, bananas, and onions have a natural barrier that can prevent pesticides from leaching into the fleshy part. Berries, apples, tomatoes, kale and other leafy greens do not. See The Dirty Dozen and the Clean Fifteen™ on page 130 for more information on this.

EAT WHOLE FOODS, NOT FAKE FOODS

Processed and packaged foods are often loaded with omega-6 fatty acids in the form of highly refined oils that can lead to chronic inflammation and serve as a precursor for a host of diseases, not to mention weight gain. These products also tend to have sneaky sugars or excess sodium that can push past the USDA daily recommended allowances. Many of these products also are made with GMO-laced corn and soy by-products, not to mention additives, chemicals, and preservatives. When you read labels with ingredients you don't recognize, stay away.

Foods to Cut from Your Diet and Kitchen

Pretty much anything in a box is off limits on the Pegan diet. That includes processed and packaged foods and processed meats such as sausage. It also means nonorganic, commercially produced cow's milk cheeses such as cheddar, Swiss, and American should be avoided, given that they are also heavily processed and loaded with hormones. It also means cutting commercially refined oils, sugars, and artificial sweeteners.

FOODS TO MINIMIZE

Sure, I like a little tofu in my salad, an occasional scoop of peanut butter, or a nice bean dip from time to time. But these and other foods, while not as damaging as sugar or margarine, have less-desirable traits, such as estrogen-triggering soy, high carbohydrates, and potential for digestive issues. They're best enjoyed in moderation.

LEGUMES

Legumes, which include beans, lentils, and peanuts, are good sources of protein, vitamins, and minerals. They also contain a lot of starch and carbohydrates, which convert to sugars in the body. If eaten in large quantities, legumes can be hard to break down before turning into fat stores. They also have naturally high levels of lectins and phytates as well as indigestible sugars, all of which can wreak digestive havoc for some.

Some Pegans maintain that lentils and garbanzo beans provide the best sources of starch and protein without all of the potentially damaging side effects. Whatever kind you prefer, Pegan guidelines suggest you enjoy no more than ½ cup a day. Note that this does not apply to fresh, organic, or sustainably grown green beans and peas, which are delicious and good for you.

Soy-Based Products

Soy is one of those highly contested ingredients. Consuming soy milk in high quantities has been linked to raised estrogen levels. Tofu is another source of controversy. While there certainly are smaller producers of organic, additive-free tofu, fermented soy products in the form of tempeh, miso, and gluten-free soy sauce are best because the fermenting process helps break down soy, which can cause digestive issues for some. On the Pegan diet, these products should be consumed only once or twice a week at most. Try omitting all soy products for the first week or two on the plan and then slowly introduce one fermented soy product at a time, making observations about how you feel before adding more.

GRAINS

Grains—whether used in flour, bread, pasta, cereal, and even in whole form—have a tendency to spike blood sugar levels. Flour alone can spike our blood sugar as much as eating a tablespoon of pure sugar. And then there's gluten to consider. If you have celiac disease, you can't have any gluten at all. Lately, the rest of the world seems to be on a gluten-free kick that has somehow justified the production and ingestion of sugary gluten-free products, which are still processed foods at their core. Even grains that are naturally gluten-free, such as rice, can still raise blood sugar to unhealthy levels.

I try not to pay attention to the USDA's recommendation for multiple servings of grains a day, because I know that was developed as a result of heavy lobbying by large agricultural and food companies. You can get most of the fiber you need just by consuming vegetables and some fruits. From time to time, however, you might enjoy a nice grain bowl to switch things up. When you do, choose more colorful grain substitutes such as quinoa, amaranth, and teff, which are actually seeds. If you're not gluten sensitive, whole-kernel rye and sorghum are also good choices. For the purpose of this beginner's guide, I've left out grain recipes, with the exception of a quinoa-based dish, because these have more carbohydrates and might slow down weight loss. As with beans, after the two-week program, you can try adding grains back to your diet one at a time, noting how you feel with each addition. The Pegan diet recommends no more than ½ cup grains per day, max.

DAIRY

Most milking cows in America are kept impregnated year-round or fed hormones so they can be milked multiple times a day. This means that when we consume most U.S.–produced cow's milk products, we're consuming naturally occurring hormones that can contribute to raised cortisol, asthma, allergies, and dull skin. And some people, myself included, are lactose sensitive or intolerant. Modern dairy-cow breeding has also caused cows to have higher levels of inflammation-causing casein, which can further lead to digestive issues.

Yogurt and kefir are a little better than milk because they contain probiotics, which promote good gut health, but only if they're consumed in moderation as well as made with grass-fed milk and no added sugars or sweeteners. To be on the safe side, try goat and sheep's milk products because they are naturally pastured animals and aren't milked year-round.

Some cheese, too, can pose issues. You can probably get away with eating small amounts of small-batch artisanal cow's milk cheese if you are aware of the production methods involved, but it's safest to stick to goat and sheep's milk cheese, enjoyed once or twice a week in small amounts.

STARCHY VEGETABLES

The Pegan diet encourages eating a wide variety of vegetables, but starchier ones should be minimized to prevent blood sugar spikes. That includes potatoes of all types, except for purple or sweet potatoes in moderation. Winter squash, like sweet potatoes, should also be consumed in moderation, or no more than ½ cup per day.

Corn also can contribute to blood-sugar spikes. Choose only organic, non-GMO corn and heirloom varieties, if you can find them, for more flavor and antioxidants without the sneaky, sugar-like effects.

HIGH GLYCEMIC INDEX FRUITS AND JUICES

Some fruits have a higher glycemic index than others. Limit fruits high in sugar such as grapes and pineapple and stick to berries and kiwi, which are loaded with vitamin C and antioxidants. But these healthier fruits should still be consumed in moderation, about no more than ½ cup per day. Personally, if I want to eat fruit, I'll eat it earlier in the day so I have a chance to burn it off before bedtime. Apples rank lower on the GI scale. Try eating them with almond butter to balance any blood-sugar boosts. And don't forget that avocado is a fruit! Avocado ranks low on the GI list, plus it's loaded with healthy fats. I enjoy a small one just about every single day.

SWEETENERS

Saccharine and aspartame, as chemical products, are just plain unhealthy. Dr. Hyman, again in *Food: What The Heck Should I Eat?*, points out that even "natural" sugar substitutes such as stevia tend to trick our brains and raise insulin and blood-sugar levels. Cane sugar, or, worse, cane syrup, are just different terms for sugar and high-fructose corn syrup. Once thought to be somewhat safe, agave syrup is no longer recommended by nutritionists due to its highly refined nature.

The same can be said for coconut and date sugars, though there is an ongoing debate as to whether their impact on blood sugar is equal to or less than that of refined cane sugar and other sweeteners. Pegan purists suggest minimizing sweeteners in general and choosing ones in their whole, natural state, such as dates, pure maple syrup, and antioxidant-rich raw honey from a small producer (see below for more information about artisan honey). After eliminating sugar for a while, you'll notice that just a little bit of these sweeteners goes a long way.

Choosing the Right Honey

About a decade or so ago, researchers discovered that the bee population in the United States was beginning to diminish. Various reasons why were suggested, including the widespread use of pesticides and even cell phones (some theorize that excess radio waves are causing bees to get lost on their way back to the hive). As a result, there has been a growth of beekeepers looking to replenish the bee population and a parallel growth in artisanal honey production. These raw honey products are loaded with antioxidants and infection-fighting antimicrobials. Heat destroys these nutrients, so that's why it's important to stick to versions labeled "raw." It's also why I try not to use honey in baking recipes. Look for artisanal honey at farmers' markets, boutique retail shops, health food stores, progressive grocery stores, and even straight from a neighbor's backyard. Visit www.honey.com for more information.

ALCOHOL

Everyone has a vice, and I fully admit this is mine. If it's yours as well, some kinds are better choices than others. Studies show that red wine, for example, has antioxidant powers due to a substance called resveratrol found in darker-hued grapes. There are also more organic and biodynamic wines on the market these days, so you can be assured that the wine wasn't produced using grapes sprayed with chemical fertilizers and pesticides. These versions also tend to be naturally lower in sugar. Some wines produced in the United States, believe it or not, have sugar added to the grapes to speed up the fermentation process.

Pegan-Friendly Beverages

- Good old filtered water

- Filtered water with a squeeze of lemon or lime

- Homemade nut milks made by soaking nuts overnight, then blending with a little filtered water and vanilla, if desired

- Coconut milk in BPA-free cans or recyclable containers

- Warm water with lemon or a little apple cider vinegar

- Coffee in moderation without sugar or sweeteners, black or with a little medium-chain triglyceride oil or unsweetened nut milk

- Green, rooibos, black, or herbal tea, without sugar or dairy

- Coconut water in moderation

- Water with electrolyte tablets

When it comes to spirits, clear liquids are best, as studies show they have less sugar overall and can have a lesser effect on blood sugar than whiskey, Scotch, and other brown spirits. Tequila, in particular, has been shown to have the lowest impact on blood sugar. Plus, it's lower in calories than vodka, which is typically produced from grains. Consider skipping the sugary margarita mix and opt for topping off your tequila with some seltzer water and a squeeze of lime, or a little muddling of mint leaves.

CHAPTER 2

Health Benefits of the Pegan Diet

There are many benefits of the Pegan diet, with weight loss being the number one positive outcome. But there are others, too, and when these things work all together, not only does that help drop the number on the scale, it aids in clearer thinking and helps lead to an overall healthier, happier life. This is no exaggeration. After years of following a Pegan lifestyle, I have been very fortunate to experience all of these benefits. Read on to learn more about the amazing health benefits this diet offers.

HELPS YOU LOSE WEIGHT, EFFORTLESSLY

That last word is no joke. Science reports that sugar and carbohydrates immediately get stored as fat if they're not used. On the flip side, healthy fats—a pillar of the Pegan diet—do not get stored as fat because they are not processed in your liver. In fact, the body prefers to use fat as an energy source over carbohydrates or simple sugars, at least for the long haul. So unless you're running marathons or working out for hours a day, you're never going to burn off those stored calories from sugar and unhealthy carbs. On top of that, many people sit at a desk all day.

However, eating the Pegan way is not just about calories in, calories out. It's more about what kind of calories and when. It's focusing on the quality of our food choices versus the quantity of our food choices. You heard it right: No calorie counting! And it really works. In the early days of putting this book together, when I took my own advice a little more closely, I lost the last few pounds I had been wanting to get rid of for a while. And they have stayed off, too.

REDUCES BELLY FAT AND MAINTAINS LEAN MUSCLE

Here's the other kicker: eating too many processed foods and not enough whole, fresh foods, as we now know, can lead to chronic inflammation in the body. Chronic inflammation not only lays the foundation for developing potentially harmful diseases, it also causes cortisol levels to spike, which can put you in a state of constant stress. The unfortunate reaction to that hormone imbalance is stored visceral fat, the bad fat that collects around major organs and expands waistlines. By focusing on a colorful variety of fresh, whole foods in their purest form while also minimizing dairy, you can prevent these hormonal shifts to reduce belly fat. And—you guessed it—by shedding belly fat, you also shed the pounds.

While exercise is not the focus of this book, adding even a minimal amount of strength training to your routine will help boost the powers of the Pegan lifestyle. You will notice more muscle definition. Compared to belly fat, lean muscle mass burns calories more efficiently throughout the day. This is imperative not just for weight loss, but for weight maintenance once you reach your goal.

A Word on Exercise

If you're new to exercise, don't sweat it—literally. Even just a little more movement every day in the form of a short, brisk walk, taking the stairs, or parking at the far end of a parking lot will speed up the weight loss process and make you feel energized. If you want to exercise more than just a little bit or explore a new regimen, think about what you have liked and disliked in the past. Or perhaps you've heard about a certain type of exercise that you would like to try. Maybe it's a more low-impact activity such as yoga, ballet barre, or Pilates. Perhaps it's high-impact exercise such as high-intensity interval training (HIIT). In combination with recovery days and slower jogs or walks, HIIT has been shown to effectively speed up weight loss efforts by allowing you to burn more calories, torch fat, and improve strength and stamina in a shorter period of time.

Many urban areas now have boutique gyms where you can purchase class passes without having to commit to a full membership. There are also countless smartphone exercise apps on the market. Both options can help offset cost while introducing more variety. I used to be a long-distance runner, clocking miles on treadmills and pounding the pavement until my knees finally gave out. Now, I find a mixture of HIIT plus lower-impact activities such as yoga and cycling help me prevent injuries and improve my muscle tone and endurance.

KEEPS CRAVINGS UNDER CONTROL

Have you ever experienced out-of-control cravings for Ben & Jerry's ice cream, pizza at any time of the day, bagels, bready sandwiches, or chocolate, chocolate, and more chocolate in any form? Admittedly, those were my crazy cravings before I shifted into a Paleo, then Pegan, lifestyle. There's a reason why these high-protein, low-carb, low- or no-sugar diets work. Carbohydrates and any form of sugar, even in the form of an artificial sweetener, cause insulin levels to spike. If you eat carbs or sugars frequently throughout the day, even if it's in the form of what is considered by some to be healthy, like orange juice, whole-wheat toast or gluten-free pasta, insulin remains high throughout the day, even at night. In incidences of prediabetes and type 2 diabetes, this can lead to insulin resistance.

For the record, vegetables are carbs, too. However, they don't have the same impact on blood sugar because of their high fiber count. That said, beans and grains are also high in fiber, but they have a lot of hard-to-burn starchy carbs, too, which is why the Pegan diet outlines optimal choices and encourages moderation in this category. Carb consumption has addiction-like characteristics; it leads to cravings for more and more carbs (so don't blame your lack of willpower). Like alcohol abuse, too much insulin can lead to a fatty liver. Double yikes.

REGULATES APPETITE

Too much insulin also causes problems with appetite control by blocking leptin in the brain. You'll think you're hungry, even if your body has all the energy it needs. By not stressing over calories and simply focusing on choosing high-quality fresh, whole foods the majority of the time, you'll see how much your body will naturally regulate your appetite every time you sit down to a meal or eat on the run. You will remember what it really feels like to be truly hungry and be able to give your body only what it needs. You will also become more familiar with what it feels like to actually be full, although the Pegan diet is about eating until you're just about full, not stuffed. And it's kind of hard to stuff yourself on broccoli, right? When your ability to perceive a sense of fullness improves, you will likely eat less in general, which, you guessed it, leads to more weight loss!

INCREASES MENTAL CLARITY AND ELEVATES ENERGY

The energy boost you'll feel when you kick processed carbs and sugars to the curb is life-changing. At least, it was for me. Two things cause this: The lack of sugar in your diet helps ward off those erratic, emotional, addiction-like behaviors and cravings for unhealthy foods; also, by increasing our intake of foods rich in omega-3 fatty acids, such as avocados, walnuts, grass-fed beef and butter, and low-mercury fish, we're actually sending energy to and feeding our brain. Neurons crave fat; when you fuel them with it, they fire better. Recent studies show that healthy fats are not just great for heart health, they are actually more important for brain and nerve health. Aside from the mental clarity you will experience, eating vegetables and other foods in their natural state will provide you with more energy to fuel your day than you ever imagined.

IMPROVES GUT HEALTH

You might be hearing more about probiotics and gut flora, and there's a reason for that. Scientists, dietitians, doctors, and nutritionists are seeing the connection between poor gut health and everything from digestive tract problems to disease development and weight gain and belly fat. These experts report that most people have low amounts of good bacteria and high amounts of bad bacteria in their intestines. That's not anyone's fault, though. It has more to do with the way food is grown in the United States and how drugs are prescribed or, perhaps, overprescribed. Soil health, especially in nonorganic plots, is not great in this country, to the extent that even organic farms have had to work hard to develop the proper levels of nitrogen to grow fruits and vegetables with nutritional adequacy.

There are toxins in many forms in the environment, from pollutants in the air you breathe to the water—including carbon-filtered water—you drink, and even from the furniture you sit on. You need more pre- and probiotics, or the good bacteria, in your gut flora to fight off these toxins and stay regular. Sure, there are probiotics in fortified dairy products such as yogurt and kefir, but these products tend to have a lot of sugar, not to mention nonpastured dairy sources. You can obtain just as many good probiotics from a wider variety of fruits and vegetables and antioxidant-rich prebiotics such as onions, leeks, garlic, and others in the allium family. I also like to take a refrigerated probiotic pill each morning on an empty stomach to ensure I'm getting all I need.

INCREASES GOOD CHOLESTEROL

It is possible that your total cholesterol level may rise after eating the Pegan way for some time, as was the case for me. That's likely due to the rise in healthy cholesterol levels (HDLs), even if the bad cholesterol levels (LDLs) stay the same or, better yet, go down. As we now know, neither saturated fat nor eggs are the villains they once were portrayed to be.

Processed foods and oils as well as sugar and processed carbs, however, have been linked to high blood pressure and unhealthy cholesterol levels, which can cause heart disease. So go ahead and eat that healthy fat; just make sure to choose pastured proteins and nontoxic fish to ensure you're getting omega-3 fatty acids, not the inflammatory omega-6 fatty acids found in meat from corn-fed animals and in processed foods.

SHARPENS YOUR PALATE

Try cutting out sugar completely for a week, and you'll notice how sickeningly sweet anything with sugar becomes, even certain fruits! This is also true of salt. When you scale back on restaurant food and cook your own meals using good-quality salt in moderation, you will soon notice how overly salty things can taste when dining out. The good news is that contemporary chefs are starting to veer away from salty toward savory and acidic flavors. After adopting the Pegan diet, even once-detested broccoli has become a favorite for me. There are so many ways to develop the flavor of food without extra salt or sweeteners. This can be achieved by adding a little extra garlic and onion, which are powerful cancer-fighting antioxidants, as well as fresh or dried herbs; spices for heat; fat in the form of healthy oils and butters; and acid in the form of roasted tomatoes, vinegar, or a splash of citrus. Nuts and seeds round out a dish with that nice crunchy texture we crave; no need to look for that in chips anymore. When combined, hitting all these senses will prove that healthy is also very delicious.

IMPROVES YOUR SKIN

This is a fun one. When I cut out sugar and unhealthy carbs, save for treats on rare occasions, I noticed that I didn't have to wear as much foundation and that my skin actually glowed and softened a little. The Pegan diet improves your skin by increasing quality fats, foods rich in Vitamin E (such as avocados), collagen in Homemade Bone Broth (page 57), pastured, bone-in meats (yes, it's OK to gnaw on a bone like our Paleo ancestors!), and beta carotene found in orange- and deep-colored vegetables.

A NEW START

Eating the Pegan way will dramatically change your life for the better. As you can see, you will not only look and feel better, you will be better equipped to tackle life's many challenges, both mentally and physically. That sounds like a tall order, but making wise food choices and refocusing your goals will free you up from all the time spent wondering what, when, and how to eat while fueling your body and brain with the ingredients they need to perform at their best level. No more yo-yo dieting and fleeting results. Your new best you will become the permanent you.

CHAPTER 3

The Pegan Jumpstart Plan

The two-week plan that follows is a fast track toward enjoying the many health benefits of the Pegan diet, with weight loss being the primary goal. During this two-week period, you will be following more stringent diet guidelines by eliminating foods that can raise your blood sugar, such as grains and legumes. Once the two weeks have passed, you may reintroduce those foods to your diet. I suggest introducing those foods one at a time and taking notes on how you feel, to avoid suddenly falling prey to crazy cravings again.

PLAN FOR SUCCESS

Following the Pegan lifestyle takes more planning, prep work, and cooking than other diets, and that is because you are truly adopting a new way of thinking about and enjoying food. I like to do most of my chopping and other prep work as well as batch cooking on the weekends so that I can enjoy quick and healthy workday lunches and easy weeknight dinners. After a while, though, all of this will become very second nature.

Once you get the hang of things and note your food preferences and routines, cooking and meal planning is very fun! It's also a great way—and perhaps the best way—to control and know exactly what you're eating. With restaurant takeout there's usually no way to know how much salt, sugar, or refined oils went into the dish or meal. Takeout can also be quite expensive. I'm not saying you will never dine out again (see Dining Out, Pegan Style, page 34), I just view dining out as more of a treat than part of my daily or regular routine. Having a stocked Pegan pantry and being prepared with simple snacks will help you manage this.

THE JUMPSTART PEGAN PANTRY

The first step in adopting a Pegan lifestyle is to stock your pantry and refrigerator with clean, healthy foods, oils, spices, and more. This is not a complete list, nor am I suggesting that you run out and buy all of these Pegan-friendly foods and ingredients tomorrow. This is a good place to start, and you can add to your pantry over time. Most of the items on the following list should be available at your local grocery store.

PRODUCE*

- Apples, red
- Artichoke hearts, water packed
- Avocados
- Baby spinach, prewashed, bagged, or fresh
- Basil, fresh
- Beets
- Bell peppers, green, red, yellow, or orange
- Berries, fresh or frozen blueberries, strawberries, raspberries, or blackberries)
- Bok choy
- Cabbage, red or napa
- Carrots

- Celery
- Chard, Swiss or rainbow
- Chives, fresh
- Cilantro, fresh
- Collard greens
- Cucumber
- Eggplant
- Garlic
- Ginger
- Green beans
- Kale
- Lemons
- Lettuce, Boston, Bibb, red leaf, or romaine
- Limes

- Mushrooms
- Olives
- Onions, yellow or red
- Oregano, fresh
- Parsley, flat-leaf
- Peppers, jalapeño or serrano
- Rosemary, fresh
- Squash, butternut, spaghetti, acorn, yellow, or summer
- Scallions
- Shallots
- Sweet potatoes
- Tomatoes, fresh
- Tomatillos
- Zucchini

* All produce listed, with the exception of avocados and onions, should come from organic sources.

CONTINUED >

MEAT AND POULTRY

- Beef, grass-fed
- Bison, grass-fed
- Butter, grass-fed
- Chicken, pastured or organic, no antibiotics
- Eggs, pastured or organic
- Game, elk or venison
- Lamb, pastured, grass-fed
- Pork, pastured or crate-free
- Turkey, pastured

SEAFOOD*

- Arctic char, wild
- Cod
- Clams, canned or fresh
- Crab, canned or fresh
- Flounder
- Herring, wild-caught
- Lobster
- Mackerel, Atlantic or Pacific
- Mussels
- Oysters
- Salmon, wild-caught, fresh or canned
- Sardines, fresh or canned
- Scallops
- Shrimp
- Snapper
- Tilapia
- Trout
- Tuna, line-caught, albacore, fresh or canned

* Be sure to source seafood that has been sustainably harvested or farmed (see page 90).

NUTS AND SEEDS

- Almond butter, raw or dry-roasted, unsalted
- Almonds, raw
- Brazil nuts, raw
- Cashew butter, roasted, unsalted
- Cashews, raw
- Chia seeds
- Flaxseeds
- Hazelnuts, raw or dry-roasted, unsalted

- Macadamia nuts, raw or dry-roasted, unsalted

- Pecans, raw, unsalted

- Pine nuts, from Italian sources only

- Pistachios, raw or dry-roasted, unsalted

- Pumpkin seeds (pepitas), raw or dry-roasted, unsalted

- Sesame seeds, toasted

- Walnut oil*

- Walnuts, whole or chopped, raw, unsalted*

*Store walnut oil and walnuts in the refrigerator or freezer, as they spoil more quickly than other nuts.

PANTRY ITEMS

- Avocado oil

- Broth or stock, unsalted

- Cacao powder, raw

- Coconut flakes, unsweetened

- Coconut oil

- Dates, Medjool

- Honey, raw, from sustainable sources (see page 12)

- Hot sauce, no additives

- Maple syrup, no additives

- Miso

- Mustard, Dijon

- Nori sheets

- Nutritional yeast

- Olive oil, extra-virgin, cold-pressed

- Salsa, no sugar or additives

- Sesame oil

- Soy sauce, gluten-free, tamari, or coconut aminos

- Sriracha

- Tempeh

- Tofu, sprouted

- Tomatoes, no sugar or salt added, crushed, chopped, or whole, boxed

- Vanilla, extra pure, no alcohol

- Vinegars, balsamic, red wine, cider, sherry, rice, coconut

- Wasabi paste

CONTINUED >

SPICES

- Bay leaves

- Black pepper or peppercorns

- Cayenne pepper

- Chili powder

- Cinnamon, ground

- Cumin, ground

- Curry powder

- Garlic powder

- Nutmeg, whole

- Onion powder

- Oregano, dried

- Paprika, hot, sweet, or smoked

- Red pepper flakes

- Salt (sea salt and pink salt are the most natural types and contain the most nutrients; kosher salt is also good)

- Thyme, dried

- Turmeric

How to Store Fresh Herbs

Store fresh herbs upright in a water-filled glass in the refrigerator so the stems can soak up the water. Using scissors, snip off the leaves as needed. Don't forget to add more water if left in the refrigerator for a few days. Herbs will last this way for about a week.

EQUIPMENT AND SUPPLIES FOR THE PEGAN KITCHEN

This first list includes must-have items for a Pegan lifestyle. That's because eating this way involves more home cooking than you may have done in the past. This is a great time to make some simple investments that will last a lifetime. The second list features nice-to-have items that you can collect over time.

MUST-HAVE

- Blender or food processor
- Cutting board
- Freezer-safe resealable plastic bags
- Glass containers for storing leftovers
- Jars for storing salad dressing and homemade condiments
- Kitchen knives, sharpened

- Large roasting pan for chicken, turkey, and roasts
- Liquid measuring containers
- Measuring cups and spoons
- Meat thermometer
- Mixing bowls
- Parchment paper or aluminum foil

- Pepper mill
- Rubber spatulas and tongs
- Stainless steel, cast iron, or ceramic pots and pans (not nonstick)
- Oven-safe metal sheet trays
- Ceramic or glass baking dishes
- Salt grinder

NICE-TO-HAVE

- Dutch oven (or other large, oven-safe pot)
- Microwave egg cooker

- Slow cooker
- Spice grinder
- Spiralizer

- Stockpot
- Wok

Pegan-Friendly Convenience Foods

Most Pegan-friendly foods will come from the produce, meat, and seafood sections of your local grocery store, also known as the outer rim. However, you can look for these items in the frozen food section and inside aisles, too.

- Almond or cashew butter, raw, unsalted

- Berries, organic and frozen for smoothies

- Bone broth or stock, unsalted, packaged in recyclable box containers or BPA-free aluminum cans

- Cauliflower and cauliflower rice, fresh or frozen

- Mayonnaise, made only with extra-virgin olive or avocado oil

- Noodles, fresh or frozen, made from spiralized zucchini or carrot

- Vegetables (not starchy), organic and frozen

THE MEAL PLAN

This 14-day plan truly is a jumpstart. In addition to adhering to Pegan guidelines, it also eliminates grains, legumes, dairy, and other high-glycemic-index foods for the two-week duration. Eliminating alcohol during this 14-day period also will speed up your weight loss goals.

For the first week, you're skipping the Grain-Free Granola (it has a touch of maple syrup) and sticking to protein-laden eggs and avocado at breakfast. Breakfast can be eaten at any time of the morning, but only when you feel hunger. You might also want to cut out any and all sweets, even the Pegan-friendly recipes in this book, for the first week or two. And, while this book contains a couple of recipes using quinoa and lentils, we're skipping them for the first two weeks to reset blood sugars and jumpstart your metabolism.

5 Pegan-Friendly Snacks

1. Hard-boiled egg or 30-Second Egg (see page 45)

2. Handful of raw nuts

3. Celery sticks spread with almond or cashew butter

4. One small or one-half large avocado, with or without hot sauce

5. Apple or kale chips with nut butter

As the Pegan lifestyle is more plant-based, most breakfasts and lunches will feature vegetables, with more meat and fish at dinner. Even if I'm cooking just for myself or for two people, I still like to make recipes that serve four so I can have leftovers at lunch or dinner for the next day or two. Also, if you plan to cut recipes in half, consider purchasing veggies from the salad bar. This will help minimize waste. This plan also assumes that you work during the week and have more time to cook on the weekends. This is when I like to make big batches of soup and bone broth, Veggie-Eggy Muffins (page 46), Overnight Chia Seed Pudding (page 43), Grain-Free Nutty Granola (page 42), Easy Cauliflower Rice (page 107), and snacks such as apple and kale chips for easy workday lunches and light dinners.

THE 14-DAY PEGAN JUMPSTART PLAN

DAY #	DAY	BREAKFAST	LUNCH	DINNER
1	MONDAY	2 Veggie-Eggy Muffins (page 46) with optional avocado and hot sauce (make on Sunday)	Chilled Asparagus Salad with Lemon Vinaigrette (page 64)	Pegan-Style Bibimbap (page 72: save extra Easy Cauliflower Rice, page 107, and veggies for days 2 and 4)
2	TUESDAY	Berry Power Smoothie (page 41)	Smoked Salmon, Cucumber, and Avocado Sushi (page 94; using leftover veggies and rice from day 1)	Roasted Chicken Thighs with Spanish-Style Romesco Sauce (page 84) with leftover Easy Cauliflower Rice
3	WEDNESDAY	Overnight Chia Seed Pudding (page 43) with Grain-Free Nutty Granola (page 42; make on Tuesday)	Easy Cucumber-Tomato Gazpacho (page 55; could make Tuesday night)	Miso-Glazed Pan-Seared Salmon with Bok Choy (page 93)
4	THURSDAY	2 Veggie-Eggy Muffins (page 46) with optional avocado and hot sauce	Leftover Roasted Chicken Thighs with Spanish-Style Romesco Sauce and leftover Easy Cauliflower Rice	Ceviche Fish Tacos with Easy Guacamole (page 96; save remaining butter lettuce for day 6)
5	FRIDAY	Berry Power Smoothie (page 41)	Broccoli Salad with Red Onion and Creamy Dijon Vinaigrette (page 62)	Marinated Flank Steaks with Cilantro Chimichurri (page 70) and Paprika-Dusted Sweet Potato Fries (page 112)
6	SATURDAY	Easy Avocado-Baked Eggs (page 45)	Butter Lettuce Salad with Quinoa, Cucumber, and Creamy Green Dressing (page 59)	Slow-Cooker Carnitas with Roasted Tomatillo Salsa (page 78; could start Friday night)
7	SUNDAY	Meat-Free Eggs Benedict with Lemon Hollandaise Sauce (page 48)	Leftover Slow-Cooker Carnitas with Roasted Tomatillo Salsa with lettuce wraps and taco fixings	Spaghetti Squash with Roasted Cherry Tomatoes and Spicy Mini Meatballs (page 74)

DAY #	DAY	BREAKFAST	LUNCH	DINNER
8	**MONDAY**	Gluten-Free Seedy Crackers (page 120; make on Sunday) spread with almond or cashew butter	Gingery Chicken Lettuce Wraps (page 86; make on Sunday)	Crab Cakes with Creamy Citrus Slaw (page 102)
9	**TUESDAY**	Berry Power Smoothie (page 41)	Roasted Beet and Kale Salad with Garlicky Dressing (page 60)	Picadillo-Stuffed Bell Peppers (page 73)
10	**WEDNESDAY**	Overnight Chia Seed Pudding (page 43) with Grain-Free Nutty Granola (page 42; make on Tuesday)	Leftover Picadillo-Stuffed Bell Peppers	Oil-Poached Whitefish with Lemony Gremolata (page 95)
11	**THURSDAY**	2 Veggie-Eggy Muffins (page 46) with optional avocado and hot sauce	Shrimp Fried Rice (page 99)	Cashew Chicken with Stir-Fried Vegetables (page 81)
12	**FRIDAY**	Two 30-Second Eggs (page 45) with optional avocado	Leftover Cashew Chicken with Stir-Fried Vegetables	Mussels with Lemon-Garlic-Herb Broth (page 100)
13	**SATURDAY**	Breakfast "Burritos" with Avocado and Pico de Gallo (page 50)	Watermelon, Avocado, and Mint Salad with White Balsamic Vinaigrette (page 63)	Sheet Pan Pork Tenderloin with Brussels Sprouts, Sweet Onion, and Rosemary (page 80)
14	**SUNDAY**	Mini Pegan Pancakes with Blueberry Syrup (page 44)	Butternut Squash and Sweet Potato Bisque (page 56)	Clam Linguine with Zucchini Noodles (page 101)

PEGAN DIET FOR LIFE

After you complete the meal plan, and possibly even after the first week, don't be surprised to find that you actually crave salads, colorful fruits and vegetables, nut butter, and iron-rich steak. This is because you're listening to your body and embracing the natural hunger rhythms and messages it's sending about what vitamins and nutrients you need.

Dining Out, Pegan Style

The 14-Day Pegan Jumpstart Plan assumes you will be making your own food, not eating out or ordering takeout, so that you're in control of the ingredients you eat. Once you're beyond the Jumpstart Plan, going out shouldn't be a problem if you follow these guidelines:

- Choose a salad, but make your own dressing by requesting olive oil and vinegar or a squeeze of lemon.

- Skip the meat at most fast-food joints, unless it's clear the protein came from a grass-fed source.

- Avoid sautéed vegetables. Ask for steamed instead to avoid the processed oil usually used in this cooking method.

- Watch out for dishes labeled "creamy," "breaded," or "crusted," as they were likely made with flour or bread crumbs.

- Know that most commercially made soups use flour, cornstarch, or other thickeners, and a high amount of salt—and not the good kind, either.

- Ask for extra lettuce and eat your grass-fed burger without the bun.

- Skip the bread basket.

The real idea behind the Pegan lifestyle is that you are in control of what you eat. If I'm generally Pegan 90 to 95 percent of the time, but I want a ridiculously cheesy pizza on a Sunday night, I will enjoy and savor every last bite of it and refuse to feel guilty about it. That said, I likely will have a salad and go for a run the next day. See where I'm going with this? The word *cheat* may have been in your food vocabulary in the past, but after you adopt a Pegan lifestyle, it should no longer be.

You might be hearing more about intermittent fasting these days. The idea behind that is that it's okay to skip breakfast or eat lunch a little later from time to time. When you choose healthy, Pegan-friendly foods, there's less need for a rigid fasting schedule, because your blood sugar level and cravings will be more stabilized. Just listen to your body and eat only when you are hungry. If that means you had dinner at 7:30 p.m. and are not hungry until 10 a.m. the next day, it's okay to have your breakfast or first meal then. Remember, you—not the sugar or the junk food—are in control.

PART II

THE RECIPES

These recipes were developed to be as delicious as possible while using fewer ingredients and cross-utilizing others. Some dishes take a touch longer to make and work best for more luxurious weekend meals or meal prepping on Sundays. However, the majority were written to be as simple as possible for quick and tasty weekday breakfasts, lunches, or dinners for busy Pegan eaters on the go. You might be surprised to see the many optional garnishes (citrus, fresh herbs, spices, hot sauces) listed with each recipe. This was deliberate, in order to make these meals as customizable as possible and offer multiple ways to infuse more flavor without any excess sodium or sweeteners.

You might find that the recipes call for a bunch of cilantro or scallions, one small or medium onion, juice from one lemon, and other less exact measurements, along with a few optional garnishes. The reason for that is not only to minimize food waste or create too many leftovers, but also to add a strong punch of flavor. When you're on the Pegan diet, you are naturally using less salt and little to no sweeteners, so it's important to develop flavor in other ways with fats, acids, spices, and herbs. These are the tools every professional chef uses in restaurant cooking. Since you're the chef now, there's no need to hold back. Be bold and enjoy. A side note: If you know you like heat or spice, feel free to increase the amount of those ingredients.

Butternut Squash and Sweet Potato Bisque (page 56)

CHAPTER 4

Breakfast & Egg Dishes

The "all-day" breakfast concept continues to trend, especially as we break down the notion that we need three square meals a day to be satisfied. This chapter includes a mix of tasty recipes to fuel your day, from protein-rich egg dishes to super-easy, set-it-and-forget-it overnight chia seed pudding, to a grain-free granola that can be prepped ahead of time to enjoy during a rushed morning or even as a mid-meal snack. No need for sugary cereal and milk. There are also some options for more luxurious, weekend brunches that take a few extra minutes to prepare, but are worth the effort.

Berry Power Smoothie

Prep time: 2 minutes | **Serves** 1

This is my go-to breakfast or meal replacement for weekdays or after a hard workout. It also serves as a nice dessert or healthy pick-me-up in the afternoon. The nut butter adds richness and healthy fat to keep you full longer. Don't worry, the use of spinach doesn't change the taste of the smoothie; rather, it adds a nice shot of extra nutrition without having to cook. Cinnamon adds even more flavor and, according to studies, helps control appetite. Feel free to add it, or not. If you don't already have a blender, now is a great time to get one.

¼ **cup frozen blueberries**

¼ **cup frozen strawberries**

½ **cup baby spinach**

2 **tablespoons unsalted almond butter**

1½ **cups coconut milk or unsweetened nut milk**

⅛ **teaspoon ground cinnamon (optional)**

Place all of the ingredients into a blender and pulse until well combined, about 1 minute. Pour into a glass and enjoy immediately.

> **INGREDIENT TIP:** Ideally, you should use frozen berries to make the smoothie cold without the need for ice, which can dilute the flavor. If you pick up some nice berries from a farmers' market, or have fresh ones on hand, you can freeze them in a single layer on a sheet pan, then transfer the frozen fruit to a resealable plastic bag for long-term storage.

PER SERVING: Calories 359; Total fat: 27g; Total carbs: 19g; Fiber: 7g; Sugar: 8g; Protein: 11g; Sodium: 129mg

Grain-Free Nutty Granola

Prep time: 7 minutes | **Cook time:** 25 minutes | **Makes** 3 cups (¼ to ½ cup per serving)

You will never go back to that super sugary, store-bought granola after trying this recipe, which delivers an option that is much more satisfying for the appetite. Feel free to eat this with sugar- and additive-free nut, coconut, sheep's, or goat's milk yogurt in the morning. It also can be enjoyed on its own at breakfast or as a quick snack at work. If you prefer raw honey as your sweetener, use it as a topping, as cooking raw honey degrades its natural antioxidative nutrients.

1½ cups chopped raw walnuts or pecans

1 cup raw almonds, sliced

½ cup seeds, toasted or roasted unsalted sunflower, sesame, or shelled pumpkin

¼ cup unsweetened coconut flakes

½ cup coconut oil or unsalted grass-fed butter, melted

1 tablespoon maple syrup

1 teaspoon alcohol-free vanilla extract

1 teaspoon ground cinnamon, or to taste

¼ teaspoon sea salt or Himalayan salt

1. Preheat oven to 300°F.
2. Line a rimmed baking sheet with parchment paper or foil.
3. Add the walnuts, almonds, seeds, and coconut flakes to a large bowl. In a separate bowl, mix the oil with the maple syrup, vanilla, cinnamon, and salt. Pour over the nut mixture, tossing to coat.
4. Spread the mixture evenly on the prepared baking sheet and bake until golden brown, about 25 minutes, stirring once halfway through. Cool completely.

INGREDIENT TIP: Walnuts are loaded with alpha-linolenic acid (ALA), a plant-based omega-3 fatty acid, and just a ¼ cup serving provides 156 percent of the daily recommended allowance. Pecans also have some of these essential fatty acids, but only a fifth of the amount in walnuts.

STORAGE: Store in an airtight container or resealable plastic bag at room temperature for a week or freeze for up to two months.

MAKE IT FASTER: Use presliced and chopped nuts.

PER SERVING: Calories 248; Total fat: 25g; Total carbs: 6g; Fiber: 3g; Sugar: 2g; Protein: 4g; Sodium: 40mg

Overnight Chia Seed Pudding

Prep time: 30 seconds | **Serves** 1

This is a tasty grain-free alternative to oatmeal that's great when topped with berries or even kiwi slices and Grain-Free Nutty Granola (see page 42). It's also super easy to make. Just add the ingredients to a jar and let the chia seeds soak up all the liquid overnight; it will be ready to eat right away in the morning. Feel free to double this recipe if you want more. Just use a bigger jar or split it into two jars so there is enough room for the chia seeds to expand.

3 tablespoons chia seeds

1 cup coconut milk or unsweetened nut milk

1 teaspoon alcohol-free vanilla extract

1 teaspoon maple syrup (optional)

1. In a large jar or bowl, combine all the ingredients, stirring to mix. Close or cover and refrigerate overnight.
2. The next day, add your preferred toppings and enjoy.

PER SERVING: Calories 293; Total fat: 19g; Total carbs: 21g; Fiber: 17g; Sugar: 1g; Protein: 10g; Sodium: 367mg

Mini Pegan Pancakes with Blueberry Syrup

Prep time: 2 minutes | **Cook time:** 10 to 17 minutes | **Makes** about 12 pancakes (3 per serving)

These gluten-free, nut-free pancakes are the perfect alternative to using any flour at all, even the Pegan-friendly kinds. With just a few ingredients, they're easy to make and perfect for a tasty weekend breakfast or brunch for yourself or the family. While bananas are a touch higher than berries on the glycemic index, you're only using one in the recipe with no sweetener added, so a little goes a long way.

1 very ripe banana

2 large eggs

1 tablespoon alcohol-free vanilla extract

1 teaspoon ground cinnamon

Pinch sea salt or Himalayan salt

¼ cup coconut oil or clarified butter (page 49), divided

2 cups fresh or frozen blueberries

1. In a medium bowl, mash the banana until softened. Add the eggs and continue to mash until smooth and most of the chunks are blended. Stir in the vanilla, cinnamon, and salt.

2. Heat 1 tablespoon of the coconut oil in a large skillet or flat cast iron pan over medium heat. Pour in 2 to 3 tablespoons of the batter to form 3-inch rounds. Cook the pancakes four at a time until set and golden brown, 2 to 4 minutes total, flipping once. Transfer to a plate to cool. Repeat until the remaining batter is used up, adding 1 tablespoon coconut oil in between each batch.

3. In a separate, small saucepan, add the blueberries and remaining 1 tablespoon coconut oil. Cook over medium heat, constantly mashing berries with a wooden spoon, until juices reduce to a syrup-like consistency, 3 to 5 minutes. Set aside to cool.

4. Serve pancakes with the blueberry syrup on the side.

STORAGE: Freeze extra pancakes, separated by parchment paper, for up to two months for a quick breakfast on the go. Blueberry syrup will keep in the refrigerator for about a week.

PER SERVING: Calories 224; Total fat: 17g; Total carbs: 18g; Fiber: 3g; Sugar: 12g; Protein: 4g; Sodium: 48mg

Easy Avocado-Baked Eggs

Prep time: 5 minutes | **Cook time:** 15 minutes | **Serves** 2 to 4

This is an easy and nutritious combination of quality protein and healthy fats to fuel your day. Top with Pegan-friendly sugar-free salsa, hot sauce, or sriracha, freshly squeezed lime juice, chopped fresh cilantro, or crunchy pepitas. This adds more acid, heat, and texture to round out the meal and satisfy your taste buds.

2 medium or large avocados, halved and pitted
4 large eggs
¼ teaspoon freshly ground black pepper

1. Preheat the oven to 425°F.
2. Scoop out some of the pulp from the avocado halves, leaving enough space to fit an egg, reserving the pulp for Easy Guacamole (see the recipe on page 96).
3. Line an 8-by-8-inch baking pan with foil. Place the avocado halves in the pan to fit snugly in a single layer, folding the foil around the outer avocados to prevent tipping.
4. Crack 1 egg into each avocado half; season with pepper. Bake, uncovered, until the whites are set and the egg yolks are cooked to your desired doneness, 12 to 15 minutes. Remove from the oven and let rest for 5 minutes before serving.

PER SERVING: Calories 433; Total fat: 37g; Total carbs: 16g; Fiber: 12g; Sugar: 1g; Protein: 16g; Sodium: 154mg

30-Second Egg

1. Crack an egg into a mug.

2. Cover with a paper towel or microwave-safe cover and microwave on high power for 30 seconds, possibly a few seconds longer if you have a low-wattage microwave.

3. Top with hot sauce or salsa and avocado for a super quick breakfast or protein- and fat-fueled snack. Note: consider purchasing a small microwaveable egg cooker instead of using a mug. There are also larger containers for making quick and easy scrambled eggs in the microwave.

Veggie-Eggy Muffins

Prep time: 7 to 10 minutes | **Cook time:** 20 minutes | **Makes** 12 muffins (1 or 2 per serving)

These are great for workweek breakfasts. I will eat two if I'm extra hungry because they only have about one egg each. Top with optional avocado, cilantro, salsa, or hot sauce to make it a more satisfying meal. I also grab one of these for a quick, protein-fueled, no-sugar snack at any time of the day. If you're a flavor-seeker, like me, and not afraid of a little heat, definitely add the jalapeño—no hot sauce needed.

Extra-virgin olive oil, coconut oil, or clarified
   butter (page 49), for greasing (optional)
12 large eggs
2 teaspoons sea salt or Himalayan salt
2 teaspoons freshly ground black pepper
1 medium red bell pepper, seeded and diced
1 medium orange, yellow, or green bell
   pepper, seeded and diced
1 cup packed baby spinach, finely chopped
½ cup thinly sliced scallions
1 small jalapeño pepper, seeded and
   minced (optional)

1. Preheat the oven to 350°F. Grease a 12-hole muffin pan or use paper muffin liners.
2. In a large bowl, place the eggs, salt, and pepper and beat until fluffy. Add the peppers, spinach, scallions, and jalapeño, stirring to combine.
3. Ladle the egg mixture evenly into the prepared muffin pan.
4. Bake until a toothpick or paring knife comes out clean when inserted, about 20 minutes. Let the muffins cool in the pan about 10 minutes before serving.

STORAGE: Store muffins in layers separated by parchment paper or foil in an airtight container in the refrigerator for 5 days to eat throughout the week.

MAKE IT FASTER: Purchase pre-diced bell peppers, if available.

PER SERVING (1 MUFFIN): Calories 83; Total fat: 5g; Total carbs: 3g; Fiber: 1g; Sugar: 1g; Protein: 7g; Sodium: 385mg

The Amazing Egg

Eggs are nutritional powerhouses. Forget about the messages of years ago falsely linking egg yolks to raised cholesterol levels. In fact, studies now show that egg yolks increase healthy cholesterol levels (HDLs) while decreasing the lousy kind (LDLs). Plus, they're packed with not just protein but also choline, which helps with muscle control, memory, and mood stabilization. Eggs also contain lutein and zeaxanthin, which help prevent cataracts and improve eye health, so you can skip the egg-white omelet in favor of whole eggs. Eggs also have 13 other essential vitamins and minerals with just 70 calories each. Unless you have an allergy to eggs or egg yolks, feel free to enjoy a couple of eggs every day. Look for pastured eggs or, at the very least, free-range and organic. A word about cage-free: This applies only to eggs, not to meat, and indicates that the eggs came from hens that were not kept in cages and free to roam, but still raised indoors in a barn. The Animal Welfare Institute points out that in some cases, these hens don't have much more space than caged birds. Pastured eggs are best, as the hens are allowed to roam outside and peck at plants and insects (which they like to do), and which increases healthy omega-3 levels, making for more golden-colored, buttery-tasting yolks.

Meat-Free Eggs Benedict with Lemon Hollandaise Sauce

Prep time: 12 minutes | **Cook time:** 6 minutes | **Serves** 2

Poaching eggs and making hollandaise takes a little extra time and care. Once you get the hang of it, it's a great go-to dish for a luxurious weekend brunch. Make sure the eggs are very cold when you poach them; this helps keep the eggs together and prevents the whites from creating too many "ribbons" when poaching.

HOLLANDAISE SAUCE:

3 large egg yolks (save whites for other use)

½ cup extra-virgin olive oil, ghee, or clarified butter (see page 49)

1 tablespoon lemon juice (from about ½ lemon)

Pinch salt

Pinch cayenne pepper

EGGS:

2 teaspoons apple cider vinegar or white vinegar

4 large eggs

1 large ripe beefsteak or heirloom tomato, ends removed, cut into 4 thick slices

1 cup baby spinach

Freshly ground black pepper

1. For the hollandaise sauce, bring a pot of water, filled to about 4 inches up the sides, to a boil. Set aside 2 tablespoons of the hot water. In a medium metal bowl, whisk the egg yolks. Add in the olive oil, hot water, lemon juice, salt, and cayenne and continue whisking. Hover the bowl over the pot of boiling water. Whisk constantly until the sauce thickens, 1 to 2 minutes, keeping the bowl from touching the boiling water, to prevent the eggs from curdling. Remove the bowl of hollandaise sauce from the pot of water, and set it aside on another part of the stovetop.

2. To poach the eggs, reduce the heat under the pot of boiling water to a simmer and add the vinegar. Prepare a paper-towel lined plate. One at a time, carefully crack the eggs into a small bowl, then use the bowl to slowly slide 2 of the eggs into the water. Simmer for 2 minutes. Using a slotted spoon, transfer the eggs to the paper towel-lined plate. Repeat the process with the remaining 2 eggs.

3. To serve, divide the tomato slices between two plates. Top each tomato with a few spinach leaves, 1 poached egg, and 2 heaping tablespoons of the warm hollandaise. Season with black pepper and serve immediately.

MAKE IT FASTER: Use 30-Second Eggs (page 45) instead of poached eggs.

PER SERVING: Calories 423; Total fat: 39g; Total carbs: 6g; Fiber: 2g; Sugar: 4g; Protein: 16g; Sodium: 242mg

How to Clarify Butter

Microwave 1 to 2 sticks of butter in a microwave-safe container (I use a glass measuring cup). Cool in the refrigerator for about 10 minutes. Scrape off the white-colored whey along the top of the melted butter, using a metal spoon. Store clarified butter in a jar in the refrigerator for about a week.

Breakfast "Burritos" with Avocado and Pico de Gallo

Prep time: 10 minutes | **Cook time:** 3 to 5 minutes | **Serves** 2

This recipe uses avocado and an easy-to-make fresh salsa, but feel free to use any stuffing of your choice for this eggy "tortilla." You can use spinach and other veggies, or caramelized onions and homemade sausage. Personally, I prefer red onion for a more colorful and flavorful pico de gallo, but feel free to swap in white for a more traditional approach.

PICO DE GALLO:

4 very ripe medium plum tomatoes, diced

½ red onion, cut into ½-inch pieces

1 small serrano pepper, seeded and minced

¼ cup chopped fresh cilantro

Juice from 1 lime

BURRITOS:

6 large eggs

½ teaspoon sea salt or Himalayan salt

½ teaspoon freshly ground black pepper

2 tablespoons unsalted grass-fed butter

1 large or 2 small avocados, peeled, pitted, and cut lengthwise into 1-inch slices

1. Make the pico de gallo first to allow the flavors to meld. In a medium bowl, toss together all the ingredients until well combined. Set aside.

2. In a large bowl, beat the eggs with the salt and pepper until fluffy. Heat the butter in a large skillet over medium-low heat until melted, then ladle in half of the egg mixture. Using a rubber spatula, spread out the egg mixture in a thin layer and allow to set on the bottom, about 1 minute. Gently flip the egg "tortilla" and continue to cook, about 30 seconds. Transfer to a plate. Repeat the process with the remaining eggs.

3. To roll the burritos, spread about 2 to 3 tablespoons of the pico de gallo down the center of each of the "tortillas," forming a line from top to bottom. Roll, starting with the filled side closest to you. Top with avocado and additional salsa, if desired, before serving.

STORAGE: Pico de gallo will keep in the refrigerator overnight, but chilling it does degrade the flavor.

MAKE IT FASTER: You might be able to find clean, Pegan-friendly pico de gallo at your local grocery store instead of making it yourself.

PER SERVING: Calories 528; Total fat: 39g; Total carbs: 25g; Fiber: 9g; Sugar: 10g; Protein: 24g; Sodium: 412mg

CHAPTER 5

Salads & Soups

Watermelon, Avocado, and Mint Salad with White Balsamic Vinaigrette, page 63

Salads and soups, as you might have guessed, offer a great way to sneak in all your veggies, but they are also culinary playgrounds for experimenting with fun flavor combinations. Though this chapter contains several recipes for both, it's easy to build a salad or soup with a wider variety of flavors and textures using Pegan-friendly foods of your choice. Here's my advice for building a better salad: start with a base (kale, romaine, broccoli), add color (roasted beets, peppers, berries), add fat and acid (avocados, tomatoes, olive oil and vinegar, pickled red onions, mustard-based dressings) and a crunchy topper (sunflower seeds, pepitas, crushed nuts). With this method you won't go wrong, as it creates a satisfying balance of flavor and texture. Same for soup: pick your style (creamy or chunky), favorite veggies (including heartier ones such as squash and sweet potato), plus another Pegan-friendly, crunchy topper.

Easy Cucumber-Tomato Gazpacho

Prep time: 5 to 7 minutes | **Serves** 2 (makes about 2 cups)

This version of gazpacho uses extra-virgin olive oil instead of cream or bread as a thickener. I like to make this in the summer when tomatoes are in peak season. Otherwise, you can use hydroponically grown tomatoes or boxed tomatoes without any added salt. Traditional gazpacho recipes call for peeled tomatoes, but the skin actually has higher concentrations of lycopene, so simply blend for a little extra nutrition. Same with the cucumber peel, which is the most nutrient-dense part of the vegetable.

8 very ripe plum or heirloom tomatoes
1 medium red bell pepper, seeded and
    coarsely chopped
1 medium cucumber, coarsely chopped
⅓ cup extra-virgin olive oil
1 tablespoon balsamic or red wine vinegar
Salt
Freshly ground black pepper
Pepitas or sunflower seeds, for garnish

1. Add the tomatoes, pepper, and cucumber to a blender or food processor and pulse a few times to break down.
2. With the motor running, add the oil and process until very smooth and velvety, at least 2 minutes. Add the vinegar and process briefly to combine.
3. Refrigerate the soup for at least 2 hours. Serve cold with salt and pepper to taste and garnish with the seeds.

> **STORAGE:** This soup will keep for up to 5 days in the refrigerator or 3 months in the freezer.
>
> **MAKE IT FASTER:** Purchase pre-chopped bell pepper and cucumber, if available.

PER SERVING: Calories 376; Total fat: 34g; Total carbs: 20g; Fiber: 5g; Sugar: 12g; Protein: 4g; Sodium: 95mg

Butternut Squash and Sweet Potato Bisque

Prep time: 7 minutes | **Cook time:** 1 hour | **Serves** 2 (makes about 3 cups)

This is my favorite soup to make on cooler days, when squash and sweet potato are in season. The addition of grass-fed butter and Homemade Bone Broth (page 57) adds richness without the need for cream or milk. Now's a great time to invest in that blender; you'll use it for many Pegan-friendly soups such as this, as well as for smoothies. Want an amazing purée as a base for seared scallops or other proteins? Simply omit the broth.

1 (2-pound) butternut squash

1½ tablespoons extra-virgin olive oil

1 medium sweet potato

¼ cup (½ stick) unsalted grass-fed butter

2 cups Homemade Bone Broth (page 57) or unsalted chicken stock, plus more as needed

¼ teaspoon salt

½ teaspoon ground cinnamon

¼ teaspoon freshly ground black pepper

2 tablespoons full-fat coconut milk, for garnish (optional)

2 tablespoons pomegranate seeds, for garnish (optional)

1. Preheat oven to 375°F.
2. Slice the squash in half and remove and discard the seeds. Place the squash, cut-side up, on a baking sheet or roasting pan and rub with the olive oil. Pierce a few holes in the sweet potato and place on the same sheet or pan. Roast until the squash and potato are very tender when pierced with a fork or knife and the squash is slightly caramelized, 50 to 60 minutes.
3. Remove from the oven, slice open the sweet potato, and let cool. When cool enough to handle, using a large metal spoon, scrape out the sweet potato and squash flesh into a food processor or blender, discarding the skin.
4. Add the butter and process a few times until melted. Add the broth, salt, and spices and purée until smooth. Add extra broth as needed to thin the soup to the desired thickness.
5. Divide the soup between bowls, drizzle each with 1 tablespoon of coconut milk (if using), sprinkle with 1 tablespoon of pomegranate seeds (if using), and enjoy!

STORAGE: Will keep in the refrigerator for 3 days; freeze for up to 2 months.

PER SERVING: Calories 571; Total fat: 34g; Total carbs: 67g; Fiber: 11g; Sugar: 15g; Protein: 10g; Sodium: 623mg

Homemade Bone Broth

Bone broth (aka unsalted stock or lightly seasoned broth, not the high-sodium broth you find at the grocery store) is all the rage these days, and for good reason: It's loaded with collagen, which is great for your joints; offers a solid protein source; fights infections and illnesses like the common cold; and even helps you achieve glowing skin, silkier hair, and stronger nails. Have a slow cooker or Instant Pot? Even better! These appliances offer a hands-off way to make both types of stock with easy cleanup. Here's a quick tutorial:

1. Save leftover bones from your chicken or beef dish.

2. Add some chopped onion, celery, and carrot (no peeling required as there is extra nutrition in the skins) or any leftover veggie scraps in your refrigerator.

3. Add a sprig of oregano and a bay leaf or two.

4. Add enough water to cover.

5. Cover and set the slow cooker on high for about 6 hours. Alternatively, set the Instant Pot to the broth setting for under an hour, or simmer uncovered in a stockpot for a few hours.

6. Skim off any residual fat, if desired. I sometimes like to stir it in for the healthy fat even if this clouds the stock.

7. Drain, cool, and chill in the refrigerator for at least an hour. If storing for long-term use, fill an ice tray with the stock and freeze. Or pour into small resealable plastic bags, lay flat on a sheet tray, and freeze. Remove from the sheet tray and stack in the freezer. Use stock to simmer lentils and quinoa, and as needed for other sauces and dishes.

TIP: You can also add a whole chicken to a slow cooker, Instant Pot, or stockpot and follow the same directions. Then, once cooked, discard the bones, shred the chicken, and save for use in a soup with the broth or for use in salads and tacos with lettuce wraps and other fixings.

Curried Coconut-Lentil Soup

Prep time: 10 minutes | **Cook time:** 20 minutes | **Serves** 4 (makes a little over 4 cups)

This hearty soup has just the right amount of lentils to fill you up with fiber and remain in the Pegan-friendly carb-counting range (½ cup cooked daily). I like to make a big batch on the weekends for a quick and hearty lunch during the week, especially when working outside the house. No need to peel the carrots first—less food waste.

1 tablespoon extra-virgin olive oil

1 small yellow onion, diced

2 garlic cloves, grated or minced

¼ teaspoon salt

¼ teaspoon freshly ground black pepper

½ teaspoon curry powder, or more, to taste

½ cup red lentils, rinsed

3 medium carrots, sliced into 1-inch pieces

1½ cups chicken or Veggie Trimmings Stock (page 61), or water

1 (14-ounce) can full-fat coconut milk

Crushed almonds, for garnish

1. In a medium saucepan, heat the oil over medium heat. Add the onion and cook until soft and translucent, about 2 minutes. Add the garlic, salt, pepper, and curry powder and cook until fragrant, 30 to 60 seconds.

2. Add the lentils and carrots and pour in the stock and coconut milk. Bring to a boil, reduce the heat, and simmer until the carrots and lentils are soft, about 20 minutes.

3. Serve as is, or purée in a blender or food processor for a creamier consistency, if desired. Garnish with almonds.

> **STORAGE:** Soup will keep for 4 days in the refrigerator, or up to 3 months in the freezer.

PER SERVING: Calories 372; Total fat: 28g; Total carbs: 27g; Fiber: 11g; Sugar: 7g; Protein: 9g; Sodium: 196mg

Butter Lettuce Salad with Quinoa, Cucumber, and Creamy Green Dressing

Prep time: 10 minutes (plus 30 minutes for chilling quinoa) | **Cook time:** 15 minutes | **Serves** 4 (makes 3 cups cooked quinoa; ½ cup per serving recommended)

While the Pegan diet allows for a daily serving of ½ cup cooked quinoa or lentils, if you're looking to cut carbs or going through the 14-day Pegan Jumpstart Plan, feel free to skip the quinoa in this salad or replace it with a Pegan-friendly protein of your choice. The avocado adds a nice creaminess without the need for dairy products.

SALAD:

2 cups water or chicken or Veggie Trimmings Stock (page 61)

1 cup quinoa

¼ teaspoon salt

¼ teaspoon freshly ground black pepper

8 cups butter lettuce leaves

1 large cucumber, diced (about 2 cups)

DRESSING:

1 ripe medium avocado

½ cup extra-virgin olive oil

¼ cup lemon juice (about 2 lemons)

¼ cup fresh parsley leaves

¼ cup fresh basil leaves

1 clove garlic, smashed

¼ teaspoon salt

¼ teaspoon freshly ground black pepper

1. In a medium saucepan, bring the water to a boil. Reduce the heat to a simmer, stir in the quinoa, cover, and cook until liquid is absorbed and the quinoa is soft and translucent, about 15 minutes. Fluff with a fork and season with the salt and pepper. Refrigerate for at least 30 minutes.

2. For the dressing, cut the avocado in half, remove the pit, and spoon the flesh into a blender or food processor. Add the olive oil, lemon juice, parsley, basil, garlic, salt, and pepper and process until smooth, adding more oil and lemon juice by the tablespoon as needed to thin the dressing to the desired consistency.

3. To serve, divide the lettuce leaves among four chilled plates or bowls. Top with the cucumber and warm or chilled quinoa. Drizzle 2 to 3 tablespoons of the dressing over each salad and serve.

STORAGE: Store cooked quinoa in the refrigerator for up to 5 days or in the freezer for up to 3 months.

SERVING TIP: Chill the plates or bowls in the freezer to keep the lettuce leaves vibrant and cold when serving.

PER SERVING: Calories 478; Total fat: 35g; Total carbs: 38g; Fiber: 7g; Sugar: 3g; Protein: 8g; Sodium: 309mg

Roasted Beet and Kale Salad with Garlicky Dressing

Prep time: 10 to 15 minutes | **Cook time:** 45 to 60 minutes | **Serves** 2 to 4

This luxurious salad can be served slightly warm on a weeknight or roasted the night before for a chilled, quick-to-assemble version, perfect for a filling lunch on the go. Sunflower seeds or pepitas add a nice crunch and dose of healthy fat. Add leftover cooked chicken for a little extra protein or serve with a meat or fish recipe to round out a meal.

6 red or golden beets (about 1½ pounds)

1 head garlic

⅓ cup plus 2 teaspoons extra-virgin olive oil, divided

1 bunch kale (or 6 to 8 cups baby kale)

2 tablespoons apple cider vinegar or red wine vinegar

½ teaspoon salt

½ teaspoon freshly ground black pepper, or to taste

¼ cup raw sunflower seeds, pepitas, or pistachios (optional)

Crumbled goat cheese (optional)

1. Preheat the oven to 375°F.
2. Slice the tops off the beets and wash thoroughly. Wrap each beet with aluminum foil and place on a baking sheet or roasting pan. Slice off the top of the garlic. Place the head of garlic in the center of a small square of foil. Drizzle 1 teaspoon of the oil over the top of the garlic and fold the sides of the foil to wrap into a ball. Set the wrapped garlic on one side of the pan with the beets. Roast until the beets are tender when pierced with a paring knife, 45 to 60 minutes. Remove from the oven, open the foil pouches, and let cool.
3. While the beets and garlic cool, tear the kale leaves off the ribs and then tear the leaves into smaller pieces. Massage the leaves with 1 teaspoon of the oil to soften and remove bitterness.
4. When cool enough to handle, peel the beets using your hands and a towel under cold running water. Cut the beets into small wedges and set aside.

5. To make the dressing, squeeze the garlic cloves into a blender. When the garlic is no longer steaming, add ⅓ cup oil, the vinegar, salt, and pepper, and purée until smooth.

6. To serve, toss the kale and beets with half of the dressing and divide among 4 shallow bowls. Top evenly with sunflower seeds or goat cheese, if desired. Season with more black pepper and enjoy.

STORAGE: Store extra dressing in a closed jar or container in the refrigerator for 2 weeks.

MAKE IT FASTER: Purchase precooked beets or skip the roasted garlic.

PER SERVING: Calories 476; Total fat: 28g; Total carbs: 51g; Fiber: 9g; Sugar: 24g; Protein: 11g; Sodium: 450mg

Veggie Trimmings Stock

Store the trimmed parts from onions and veggies in a resealable plastic bag in the refrigerator for a delicious veggie broth and to cut down on food waste. At the end of the week or on the weekend, add 2 cloves smashed garlic, 2 bay leaves, and the veggies to a slow cooker, Instant Pot, or Dutch oven and fill with enough water to cover. Slow cook for 6 hours, set the Instant Pot to the broth setting, or simmer over medium heat, uncovered, for 3 hours. Follow directions for Homemade Bone Broth (see page 57) to store veggie stock.

Broccoli Salad with Red Onion and Creamy Dijon Vinaigrette

Prep time: 5 minutes | **Serves** 2 to 4 (makes 4 cups)

A traditional broccoli salad has cranberries or raisins, sugar, and mayonnaise in the recipe, but this Pegan version uses red onion and Dijon mustard for some sweetness and creaminess. After the 14-day Pegan Jumpstart Plan, feel free to add some chopped Medjool dates to the recipe. I like to make this on the weekends or early in the week for an easy midweek lunch, quick snack, or side dish at dinner.

DRESSING:

⅓ cup extra-virgin olive oil

2 tablespoons apple cider vinegar

1 teaspoon Dijon mustard

¼ teaspoon salt

¼ teaspoon freshly ground black pepper

BROCCOLI SALAD:

4 cups broccoli florets

½ cup finely diced red onion

¼ cup raw or roasted unsalted sunflower seeds

1. In a large bowl, add the dressing ingredients and whisk until creamy.
2. Add the broccoli, onion, and sunflower seeds, tossing to coat.
3. Refrigerate for at least 1 hour, up to overnight.

STORAGE: Salad will keep in the refrigerator for up to 2 days.

MAKE IT FASTER: Make the salad on Sunday for a Monday or Tuesday lunch.

VARIATIONS: Use Quick-Pickled Red Onions (page 115) in place of the raw onion. Add cooked bacon for smokiness. You can always replace the sunflower seeds with sesame seeds, pistachios, or other nuts and seeds.

PER SERVING: Calories 402; Total fat: 37g; Total carbs: 16g; Fiber: 6g; Sugar: 5g; Protein: 7g; Sodium: 382mg

Watermelon, Avocado, and Mint Salad with White Balsamic Vinaigrette

Prep time: 10 minutes (plus 30 minutes for chilling) | **Serves** 2 to 4

This refreshing salad is perfect for a warm summer day when watermelon is in season. Watermelon has a low GI when eaten in small portions and balanced with other, low-GI foods. For the dressing, I like to use a good-quality aged white balsamic vinegar, which is becoming easier to find in grocery stores. If you can't find it, substitute regular balsamic vinegar or red wine vinegar. Instead of adding salt to the dressing, I like to sprinkle a little coarsely ground sea salt or pink salt over the salad to add texture as well as flavor.

⅓ cup extra-virgin olive oil

2 tablespoons white balsamic vinegar

4 cups cubed seeded watermelon (from a 4-pound watermelon)

1 ripe large avocado, pitted, peeled, and cubed

½ cup chopped fresh mint

¼ teaspoon sea salt or pink salt, or to taste

¼ teaspoon freshly ground black pepper, or to taste

½ cup crumbled goat cheese (optional)

1. In a large bowl, whisk together olive oil and vinegar. Add the watermelon, avocado, and mint, and gently toss to coat. Cover and refrigerate for at least 30 minutes to marinate.

2. To serve, divide the salad among chilled bowls or plates, season with the salt and pepper, sprinkle with the goat cheese (if using), and enjoy.

> **STORAGE:** Salad will keep in the refrigerator for 1 day but will get soggy after that.
>
> **MAKE IT FASTER:** Purchase precut watermelon.
>
> **INGREDIENT TIP:** Seek out watermelon from your local farmers' market in the summer. Once you have a taste of watermelon in peak season, it's hard to go back to anything else.

PER SERVING: Calories 555; Total fat: 48g; Total carbs: 37g; Fiber: 9g; Sugar: 23g; Protein: 4g; Sodium: 69mg

Chilled Asparagus Salad with Lemon Vinaigrette

Prep time: 5 minutes | **Cook time:** 5 minutes | **Serves** 2 to 4

Asparagus tastes amazingly refreshing and sweet when in season in the spring, and especially when eaten cooked and cooled. The idea is not to overcook it so there's still a bit of a crunch; note that farmers' market–sourced and thinner stalks of asparagus will cook much faster, in about a minute. The lemon vinaigrette offers even more brightness for a light lunch or fun side.

1 bunch asparagus, woody ends trimmed

3 tablespoons extra-virgin olive oil

Grated zest from 1 lemon

2 tablespoons lemon juice

2 teaspoons Dijon mustard

¼ teaspoon salt

¼ teaspoon freshly ground black pepper

Pinch red pepper flakes (optional)

Sunflower seeds, for garnish

1. Bring a large pot of salted water to a boil. Add asparagus and boil until bright green and crisp tender, 2 minutes. Drain and immediately rinse under cold running water or submerge in an ice bath until cool. Transfer to the refrigerator to cool completely, 30 minutes.

2. To make the dressing, vigorously whisk together the remaining ingredients (minus the seeds) until emulsified, or shake in a closed jar.

3. To serve, divide asparagus among plates and drizzle with 2 tablespoons of the dressing. Garnish with seeds for crunch or with Quick-Pickled Red Onions (page 115) if you have them on hand.

STORAGE: Dressing will keep in a jar or other closed container for 2 weeks. If it's just you or two people, you can always make the whole recipe and take the salad to work the next day; toss with the dressing right before eating.

MAKE IT FASTER: Use leftover grilled or cooked asparagus from another dish that has been chilled in the refrigerator, or purchase grilled asparagus from the prepared food section of your grocery store.

PER SERVING: Calories 207; Total fat: 22g; Total carbs: 5g; Fiber: 2g; Sugar: 2g; Protein: 3g; Sodium: 353mg

CHAPTER 6

Meat & Chicken

Picadillo-Stuffed Bell Peppers, page 73

P egan does not mean strict vegan; the diet allows meat in moderation. However, the most important thing to note is that when you *do* decide to eat meat, make sure you're choosing the best, most sustainably raised kind you can. That means, ideally, pastured chicken, heritage pork, and grass-fed beef, to avoid unnecessary antibiotics or hormones that were either given to the animals or added to the food they ate. This also ensures the animals were raised well, which helps enhance their nutrition profile and taste.

When it comes to poultry, if you can't find pastured, go for organic so as to at least avoid ingesting the same GMO- and pesticide-laced feed that the birds did. Some major grocery stores now include more information about the meat they offer. You can also ask the butcher. Be careful of labels, as noted in chapter 1. "Natural" doesn't mean anything. For the record, federal laws prohibit the use of hormones with chicken, so any poultry product labeled hormone-free also means nothing.

Grass-Fed and Pastured Meats

We are what we eat, but we are also what what we eat eats.

This couldn't be closer to the truth, especially when it comes to the meat and even fish we choose. As strict veganism grows in popularity, meat, and red meat in particular, continues to get shunned with myths that it causes cancer and heart disease. Thanks to modern studies, it is now common knowledge that meat in general does not necessarily cause these problems; rather, it's the quality of the meat that matters.

In fact, meat has been an important part of our ancestral diet, providing strong sources of protein, CLA (conjugated linoleic acid), omega-3s, and minerals such as potassium, phosphorus, zinc, iron, and vitamin B_{12}, the latter of which can only be absorbed by eating meat. But there are many problems with today's commercially produced beef and poultry. Not only are they injected with antibiotics and, in some cases, hormones, but they typically are fed an unhealthy diet of GMO-laced corn, soy, and grain products, along with many scary fillers, such as ground-up feathers, recycled animal waste, even plastic, and, in some cases, straight-up candy. This makes these animals more likely to harbor foodborne illnesses. When you eat them, you ingest everything they did.

Sourcing grass-fed beef and pastured poultry is the best way to ensure you are enjoying the highest-quality protein available. When animals are allowed to roam stress-free and enjoy the foods they were meant to eat, they are stronger and healthier, and this has a direct impact on the healthy fats and vitamins they can offer. Grass-fed beef has naturally higher levels of omega-3 fatty acids and lower levels of inflammation-causing omega-6 fatty acids, which are very prevalent in mass-produced beef. Grass-fed beef products also have higher levels of those important vitamins and minerals previously mentioned.

When it comes to pork, sourcing heritage varieties ensures that the pigs were raised outdoors on grassy fields in a humane way. Look for specific heritage varieties such as Berkshire, Chester White, Hampshire, Duroc, Guinea Hog, and others. Always know your farmer, if you can. These pork products also have higher fat levels, making them not only good sources of healthy fat but much more delicious than the "other white meat" products of the 1980s and '90s.

Marinated Flank Steaks with Cilantro Chimichurri

Prep time: 50 minutes | **Cook time:** 10 minutes | **Serves** 4

This is my go-to dish for outdoor grilling or even a weeknight dinner using the broiler. Flank steak is a leaner cut, so marinating it helps tenderize any toughness while infusing more flavor. I highly recommend making the chimichurri a day or two before making this recipe because the flavors meld together and grow stronger overnight. Also, I added a little spinach to the chimichurri to beef up the nutrients (no pun intended). Since this Argentinian condiment is typically made with parsley, feel free to use that herb instead of cilantro. Also, swap the flank steak for skirt steak if you can find it and if you prefer that cut. Pair with any veggie side, or with lettuce wraps to eat like tacos.

MARINADE AND STEAK:

1 pound flank steak

⅓ cup extra-virgin olive oil

2 cloves garlic, minced

3 tablespoons red wine vinegar or apple cider vinegar

2 tablespoons soy sauce

½ teaspoon salt

½ teaspoon freshly ground black pepper

½ teaspoon ground cumin

CILANTRO CHIMICHURRI:

1 bunch fresh cilantro

1 cup baby spinach

½ cup extra-virgin olive oil

3 tablespoons red wine vinegar or apple cider vinegar

2 cloves garlic, peeled

¾ teaspoon red pepper flakes

½ teaspoon ground cumin

Pinch salt

1. In a shallow dish or resealable plastic bag, combine the meat with the oil, garlic, vinegar, and soy sauce. Turn to coat, cover or close, and refrigerate for at least an hour or up to overnight. In a small bowl, mix together the salt, pepper, and cumin and set aside.

2. To make the chimichurri, lop off the cilantro stems with a sharp knife. Add the cilantro leaves to a food processor and pulse a few times to coarsely chop. Add the remaining ingredients and pulse until finely chopped. Alternatively, finely chop all ingredients with a knife and stir to combine.

3. For the steak, set up your grill so there is a direct heat and an indirect heat (cooler) area. Preheat the grill to medium-high heat.

4. Remove the steak from the marinade and gently shake off the excess. Rub the steaks with the salt, pepper, and cumin. Place the steak on the hot side of the grill and sear until browned, about 2 minutes per side. Move the steak to the cooler side of the grill, cover, and continue to cook until the meat is pink in the center for medium-rare doneness, flipping once, about 6 minutes total, or to your desired degree of doneness. Alternatively, cook the steak in a broiler on high until medium-rare doneness, 4 to 5 minutes per side.

5. Using a sharp or serrated knife, slice the steak against the grain at a steep diagonal angle into 1-inch-thick slices. Divide among four plates and top with the chimichurri. Serve with Easy Cauliflower Rice (see page 107), lettuce wraps, or any other veggie side.

> **STORAGE:** Leftovers will keep in the refrigerator for about a week; pair with eggs, fish, and veggies. It also goes great with Perfectly Sautéed Mushrooms with Rosemary and Baby Greens (page 110).

PER SERVING: Calories 423; Total fat: 36g; Total carbs: 2g; Fiber: 0g; Sugar: 0g; Protein: 25g; Sodium: 272mg

Pegan-Style Bibimbap

Prep time: 1 hour | **Cook time:** 5 minutes (not including Easy Cauliflower Rice) | **Serves** 4

For a vegan version of this classic Korean comfort food, use tempeh or mushrooms instead of meat, and follow the steps for the marinade. Don't forget to break the runny egg right away to bind everything together.

MEAT AND MARINADE:

1 pound grass-fed sirloin steaks, very thinly sliced

1 small bunch scallions, green and white parts, thinly sliced

¼ cup tamari or gluten-free soy sauce (plus more for vegetables)

2 teaspoons grated or minced fresh ginger

1 teaspoon maple syrup or artisanal honey

2 cloves garlic, minced

½ teaspoon red pepper flakes

1 tablespoon coconut oil or extra-virgin olive oil

CAULIFLOWER RICE AND VEGGIES:

4 cups Easy Cauliflower Rice (page 107)

1 cucumber or zucchini, cut into matchsticks

1 carrot, peeled and cut into matchsticks

¼ cup bean sprouts (optional)

OPTIONAL GARNISHES:

Toasted sesame seeds

Sesame oil

Sriracha

30-Second Egg (see page 45)

1. Into a shallow bowl or resealable plastic bag, place the steaks and marinade ingredients, except for the coconut oil, setting aside one quarter of the sliced scallions for garnish; toss to coat. Cover or close and refrigerate for 30 minutes or longer, up to overnight.

2. To cook the meat, heat the coconut oil in a large skillet over medium-high heat until melted. Add the meat and cook, stirring and flipping frequently, until just slightly pink in the center, about 5 minutes.

3. Divide the Easy Cauliflower Rice among 4 large bowls, pushing the rice to one side of the bowl. Add the zucchini and carrot matchsticks, standing them up, to another quarter of the bowl. Add the meat to another quarter and the bean sprouts (if using), to another quarter.

4. Garnish with the reserved scallions; if you like, also sprinkle with toasted sesame seeds, give a drizzle of sesame oil and/or sriracha, top with a runny egg, and enjoy.

STORAGE: Extras will keep in the refrigerator for a couple of days.

MAKE IT FASTER: Marinate the meat the night before.

PER SERVING: Calories 338; Total fat: 20g; Total carbs: 14g; Fiber: 4g; Sugar: 6g; Protein: 27g; Sodium: 1106mg

Picadillo-Stuffed Bell Peppers

Prep time: 10 minutes | **Cook time:** 15 to 20 minutes | **Serves** 2

There are many variations of picadillo in Latin American cuisine, but this Pegan version skips the starchy potatoes and sugary raisins for the sweet and savory combination of cumin and cinnamon, paired with tomato and green olives. Only cooking for one or two? Save extra stuffed peppers for a quick lunch or dinner in the next couple of days.

2 red, yellow, orange, or green bell peppers

3 tablespoons extra-virgin olive oil, divided

1 pound ground chicken or ground grass-fed beef

1 tablespoon ground cumin

1 tablespoon chili powder

1½ teaspoons ground cinnamon

¼ teaspoon salt

¼ teaspoon freshly ground black pepper

Pinch cayenne pepper (optional)

1 small yellow or sweet onion, diced

2 cloves garlic, minced

6 plum tomatoes, diced, juices reserved

1 cup pitted or pimento-stuffed green olives, quartered

½ cup chopped fresh cilantro

1. Preheat the oven to 400°F.
2. Slice the peppers in half, keeping the stem intact, and remove seeds. Lightly coat with 1 tablespoon olive oil and place on an aluminum foil–lined baking sheet, cut-side up.
3. In a medium bowl, mix the meat with the cumin, chili powder, cinnamon, salt, black pepper, and cayenne (if using).
4. Heat 1 tablespoon of the oil in a large skillet over medium heat. Add the meat and cook until lightly browned but not cooked through, about 2 minutes. Transfer to a bowl using a slotted spoon.
5. In the same skillet, heat the remaining 1 tablespoon oil. Add the onion and cook until soft and translucent, stirring a few times, about 2 minutes. Add the garlic and cook until fragrant, about 30 seconds.
6. Stir in the tomatoes and their juices, olives, and cilantro. Spoon the mixture into the bell pepper halves.
7. Bake until the peppers are tender and any excess tomato juices have evaporated, 10 to 15 minutes. Remove from the oven, allow to cool slightly, and serve.

VARIATIONS: Serve over Easy Cauliflower Rice (page 107) or with lettuce wraps; use any color bell pepper you prefer.

PER SERVING: Calories 768; Total fat: 49g; Total carbs: 29g; Fiber: 9g; Sugar: 13g; Protein: 51g; Sodium: 1308mg

Spaghetti Squash with Roasted Cherry Tomatoes and Spicy Mini Meatballs

Prep time: 10 to 15 minutes | **Cook time:** 10 to 12 minutes | **Serves** 4

This is one of my favorite go-to weeknight meals because the spaghetti squash can be cooked ahead of time, and it cooks just fine in the microwave. Plus, baking the meatballs and tomatoes makes for an easy dinner. I choose 80 percent lean beef for this recipe to prevent the meatballs from being too dry. And, because the meat is grass-fed, you'll reap the benefits of the omega-3 fatty acids.

1 (4- to 5-pound) spaghetti squash

1 teaspoon dried oregano

1 teaspoon dried thyme

1 teaspoon onion powder

1 teaspoon garlic powder

½ teaspoon freshly ground black pepper

½ teaspoon red pepper flakes

¼ teaspoon salt

1 large egg

1 pound grass-fed ground beef
  (80 percent lean)

1 pint cherry or grape tomatoes, halved

3 tablespoons extra-virgin olive oil, divided

Torn or chiffonaded fresh basil leaves,
  for garnish

1. Using a sharp knife, carefully slit a few holes in the squash. Microwave on high until tender, about 10 minutes.

2. Preheat the oven to 375°F. Line a rimmed baking sheet with aluminum foil so that it comes up on the sides.

3. In a large bowl, combine all of the spices and the salt. Add the egg and whisk to combine. Add the beef and gently mix until just combined. Do not overmix.

4. Shape the mixture into golf ball–size meatballs (about 16 total) and place on the prepared baking sheet. Toss the tomatoes with 1 tablespoon of the oil and arrange around the meatballs. Bake until just cooked through, 10 to 12 minutes.

5. Slice the squash in half crosswise (see Ingredient Tip), then scoop out and discard the seeds. Use a metal serving spoon or fork to rake the flesh inside the skin into strands and place in a large bowl. Toss with the remaining 2 tablespoons oil.

6. To serve, divide the squash strands evenly among four bowls or plates. Top each with four meatballs. Briefly mix the tomatoes and juices on the baking sheet to make a sauce and carefully pour over the top of each serving. Season with more black pepper, if you like, garnish with basil, and serve.

PER SERVING: Calories 480; Total fat: 32g; Total carbs: 30g; Fiber: 1g; Sugar: 4g; Protein: 24g; Sodium: 269mg

STORAGE TIP: Freeze any extra cooked meatballs (or make a double batch) for up to 2 months for a quick and easy weeknight dinner. When reheating, toss with a little sauce or broth to prevent them from drying out.

INGREDIENT TIP: The strands in a spaghetti squash wind around crosswise, not lengthwise, so for the longest strands, you want to cut it across its midsection, not stem to stern.

MAKE IT AHEAD: The spaghetti squash can be cooked, tossed in the olive oil, and refrigerated in an airtight container for up to 2 days. Reheat in the microwave for 1 to 2 minutes on high before topping with the meatballs and sauce.

VARIATION: You also can roast or grill the spaghetti squash. Slice the squash in half, spoon out and discard seeds, drizzle with 1 tablespoon oil and roast cut-sides down in a 350°F oven until tender, 45 to 50 minutes. Follow the same method to prepare squash before grilling over medium heat for about 20 to 25 minutes.

Brined Pork Chops with Caramelized Apple-Onion Relish

Prep time: 15 minutes, plus 1 hour for brining | **Cook time:** about 20 minutes |
Serves 2 (makes a little over 1 cup relish)

This sweet and savory pork dish is super comforting, especially on a cooler day when apples are in season. I try and source pork chops from my local farmers' market, because I know the farmer raises the animals on pasture. However, more grocery stores are carrying high-quality pork products, such as Niman Ranch. The combination of high-quality pork and brining helps prevent overcooking. Don't be alarmed by the salt content of the brine; it is used as a tenderizer along with the apple cider vinegar. I leave the skin on the apples and don't overcook them, to preserve their fiber, crunch, and low-medium glycemic index number.

BRINED PORK:

1½ cups water

½ cup apple cider vinegar

2 tablespoons salt, plus more for seasoning

1 teaspoon freshly ground black pepper (or ½ tablespoon peppercorns), plus more for seasoning

1 teaspoon maple syrup

2 (2-inch-thick) bone-in pastured pork chops

RELISH:

1 medium red apple

1 teaspoon lemon juice

2 tablespoons unsalted grass-fed butter

1 tablespoon olive oil

1 medium yellow onion, diced

2 cloves garlic, minced

2 tablespoons chopped fresh parsley (optional)

1. In a large shallow bowl, combine the water, vinegar, salt, pepper, and maple syrup and microwave on high until the salt dissolves, about 1 minute. Add the pork, submerging it in the brine. Cover and refrigerate for at least an hour and up to overnight.

2. Place a baking sheet or broiler pan in the oven and set the broiler to high. Remove the chops from the brine, shaking off any excess and patting dry. Season each side evenly with salt and pepper and set aside to dry out further while you prepare the relish.

3. For the relish, dice the apple and toss with the lemon juice. Heat the butter and oil in a medium skillet over medium heat. Add the onion and cook, stirring occasionally, until it starts to caramelize, 7 to 10 minutes. Add the garlic and cook until fragrant, about 30 seconds. Reduce the heat to low, add the apple, stir to coat with the mixture, cover the pan, and cook until just warmed, 1 to 2 minutes. Remove from the heat, stir in the parsley (if using), and set aside.

4. Transfer the pork chops to a baking sheet or broiler pan and broil until slightly pink in the center, about 3 minutes per side, reserving juices from the pan. Let rest for 3 minutes.

5. To serve, divide the chops between two plates. Pour any juice from the pan over the chops, top evenly with the apple-onion relish, and serve.

STORAGE: Extra apple-onion relish will keep in the refrigerator for up to 3 days.

INGREDIENT TIP: Studies show that onions, garlic, and other members of the allium family have the highest levels of cancer- and free-radical–fighting antioxidants among all vegetables. Use them liberally in your cooking for extra flavor and nutrients.

MAKE IT FASTER: Brine the pork the night before. The apple-onion relish also can be made ahead and gently warmed on a stovetop or in the microwave for 1 minute on 50 percent power.

PER SERVING: Calories 444; Total fat: 28g; Total carbs: 25g; Fiber: 4g; Sugar: 17g; Protein: 25g; Sodium: 651mg

Slow-Cooker Carnitas with Roasted Tomatillo Salsa

Prep time: 20 to 25 minutes | **Cook time:** 4 to 8 hours | **Serves** 4 (plus some left over)

If you have a slow cooker or Instant Pot, this is a super easy, hands-off Pegan-friendly meat dish. When served with all the optional fixings, it feeds a crowd. If you don't have these appliances, you can brown and braise the pork in a large, covered Dutch oven at a slow simmer over medium heat until tender, about 3 hours. Although I have an Instant Pot that can cook the pork in just 40 minutes at high pressure, I actually prefer using the slow cooker setting because it creates a juicier, more tender dish. Also, I like to cook the meat with the bone on for more flavor, healthy fat, and collagen, but boneless works just as well, too.

CARNITAS:

1 (2-pound) boneless pork shoulder

1 teaspoon salt

1 teaspoon freshly ground black pepper

1 tablespoon extra-virgin olive or avocado oil

2 teaspoons ground cumin, or to taste

2 teaspoons garlic powder, or to taste

2 teaspoons onion powder, or to taste

2 teaspoons chili powder, or to taste

Juice from 2 limes

ROASTED TOMATILLO SALSA:

1 pound tomatillos, husks removed, rinsed

1 small or ½ large white onion, halved

1 to 2 jalapeño or serrano peppers

1 clove garlic, peeled

1 bunch fresh cilantro

Juice from 1 lime

OPTIONAL FIXINGS:

Lettuce leaves

Cubed avocado or Easy Guacamole (page 96)

Chopped cilantro

Chopped tomatoes or Pico de Gallo (page 50)

Lime wedges

1. Cut the pork into large cubes to reduce cooking time and rub with the salt and pepper.

2. In a large skillet, cast iron pan, or Dutch oven, heat the oil. Add the pork and cook until just browned on all sides, 5 to 7 minutes, working in batches as needed to not overcrowd the pan. Transfer the pork to a slow cooker, if using. Add the cumin and garlic, onion, and chili powders and toss to coat. Add the lime juice, place the lid on the slow cooker, and set the cook time on low heat for 8 hours or high heat for 4 to 5 hours.

3. To make the salsa, preheat the broiler to high.

4. Place the tomatillos, onion (cut-side up), and peppers on a baking sheet lined with enough aluminum foil to cover the sides and catch the juices. Broil until the tomatillos are tender and the onion and peppers are slightly blackened, flipping once, 5 to 7 minutes.

5. Remove the pan from the oven, cover with a kitchen towel, and let cool, about 5 minutes. When cool enough to handle, run the peppers under cold water, remove the stems, peel off the skin, and pull out the seeds and discard. Transfer to a blender.

6. Carefully lift the foil and pour the roasted ingredients and tomatillo juices into the blender. Add the cilantro and lime juice and process until blended but still slightly chunky. Pour into a bowl or jar and refrigerate until ready to use.

7. Shred the cooked pork using two forks. Serve with salsa and optional fixings.

STORAGE: Leftover cooked carnitas will keep in the refrigerator for 3 days or freezer for up to 2 months. The salsa will last about a week in the refrigerator, or can be frozen up to 2 months.

INGREDIENT TIP: Use caution when handling jalapeños, because their heat level can vary widely. If, after cutting it in half you notice it tickles your nose when you smell it, that means it might be a hot one. Feel free to use just half if you're not a fan of a lot of heat.

MAKE IT FASTER: Cook carnitas overnight or prepare in the morning for an awesome dinner later that evening.

PER SERVING: Calories 377; Total fat: 27g; Total carbs: 8g; Fiber: 2g; Sugar: 1g; Protein: 26g; Sodium: 490mg

Sheet Pan Pork Tenderloin with Brussels Sprouts, Sweet Onion, and Rosemary

Prep time: 10 to 15 minutes | **Cook time:** 25 minutes | **Serves** 4

I don't eat pork that often, but when I do, this is a great recipe for an easy weeknight dinner because everything cooks in one pan (lining the pan first makes for easy cleanup). When choosing meat, look for pastured or crate-free organic pork.

PORK:

1 (1-pound) pork tenderloin

1 teaspoon salt

1 teaspoon freshly ground black pepper

1 teaspoon paprika (regular or smoked, optional)

BRUSSELS SPROUTS:

1 pound Brussels sprouts, trimmed and halved

1 medium yellow or sweet onion, cut into ½-inch wedges

2 tablespoons extra-virgin olive oil

1 teaspoon maple syrup

1 tablespoon fresh rosemary, minced

1. Preheat the oven to 425°F. Line a baking sheet with aluminum foil or parchment paper.

2. Place the pork in the center of the prepared baking sheet and pat dry. Mix the salt, pepper, and paprika (if using) together in a small bowl. Rub it all over the pork.

3. In a medium bowl, toss the Brussels sprouts and onion with the oil, maple syrup, and rosemary. Spoon the mixture around the pork.

4. Roast the pork and Brussels sprouts until the pork is brown outside and slightly pink inside (internal temperature should be 145°F). Remove from the oven and let rest for 3 minutes.

5. Divide the vegetables evenly among four plates. Slice the pork into 1½-inch-thick pieces and top each plate with three or four pieces.

INGREDIENT TIP: To quickly remove rosemary leaves from their stems, hold the stem from one end in one hand, and squeezing with your thumb and index finger, pull down on the needles to remove them from the stem.

MAKE IT FASTER: Pork can be rubbed with the salt, pepper, and rosemary and refrigerated overnight to further tenderize.

PER SERVING: Calories 292; Total fat: 12g; Total carbs: 15g; Fiber: 6g; Sugar: 5g; Protein: 34g; Sodium: 676mg

Cashew Chicken with Stir-Fried Vegetables

Prep time: 15 to 20 minutes | **Cook time:** 20 minutes | **Serves** 2

This is a great recipe for an easy and well-balanced weeknight meal that also packs up well for lunch the next day. If you don't already own a wok, now might be the time to invest in one. The unique shape allows for better heat circulation during high-heat cooking such as stir-frying. It also makes it easier to continuously toss the ingredients while cooking to speed up the cooking process and ensure uniformity. Once you have a great wok, making veggie-rich stir-fry will be a breeze. No need to soak the raw cashews for easier digestion since you will be toasting them in the cooking process. This dish is also delicious when served over Easy Cauliflower Rice (page 107).

2 boneless skinless chicken breasts

3 tablespoons sesame oil, divided

2 cloves garlic, minced, divided

3 tablespoons gluten-free soy sauce, tamari, or coconut aminos, divided

3 tablespoons apple cider, rice, or coconut vinegar, divided

2 tablespoons minced fresh ginger, divided

3 scallions, thinly sliced, green and white parts separated, divided

1 cup raw cashews

1 medium red, orange, or yellow bell pepper, seeded and diced

1 cup snow peas, trimmed

Red pepper flakes, to taste (optional)

1. Cut the chicken breasts into 2-inch strips. In a large shallow bowl, whisk together 1 tablespoon of the sesame oil, half of the garlic, 2 tablespoons of the soy sauce, 2 tablespoons of the vinegar, 1 tablespoon of the ginger, and half of the scallion whites and greens. Add the chicken and turn to coat. Cover and refrigerate for at least 15 minutes while preparing the rest of the stir-fry ingredients, or up to overnight.

2. Heat a dry wok or large skillet over medium-high heat. Add the cashews and cook, stirring, until fragrant and lightly toasted, 1 minute. Remove the cashews from the pan to prevent burning and set aside.

> **CONTINUED ON NEXT PAGE**

Cashew Chicken with Stir-Fried Vegetables

> CONTINUED

3. Drain the chicken, discarding the marinade, and pat dry. Add 1 tablespoon of the sesame oil to the wok or skillet, still on medium-high heat. When the oil is hot, add the chicken and cook, tossing continuously, until cooked through, about 5 minutes. Transfer to a plate or chopping board.

4. Add the remaining 1 tablespoon sesame oil, the bell pepper, and snow peas and cook, tossing continuously, until tender, about 5 minutes. Add the remaining scallion whites and remaining ginger and cook until just fragrant, about 1 minute. Return the chicken and cashews to the pan. Add the remaining 1 tablespoon soy sauce and vinegar, and the red pepper flakes (if using). Toss to combine. Serve garnished with the reserved scallion greens.

STORAGE TIP: Pack up leftover stir-fry for a weekday lunch the next day; stir-fry will keep for up to two days in the refrigerator. Eats just as well cold or reheated.

MAKE IT FASTER: Use pre-diced bell peppers or a packaged stir-fry mix and minced garlic and ginger, if available.

PER SERVING: Calories 774; Total fat: 49g; Total carbs: 36g; Fiber: 7g; Sugar: 7g; Protein: 49g; Sodium: 1463mg

Buying Poultry

Labels using the terms "natural" and "antibiotic-free" are pretty much worthless, because most chickens in the United States are raised indoors and likely fed GMO-laced soy and grains. If it's labeled organic, it means the chickens were fed a diet of organic grains. Still, chickens like to roam outside and peck at the ground for plants and insects. Free-range might sound as if they're allowed to do this, but Animal Welfare Certified representatives report that the rules have bent a little for those labels, and there is no way to know how much access to the outdoors the birds had. It could have been hours, or even just minutes.

Pastured is the most Pegan-friendly label for poultry, because it implies that the birds were outside longer and allowed to peck at the ground; however, it's a premium product that can be challenging to find. Many local farms bringing poultry to farmers' markets won't have this label, but if you talk to them about their farming methods, you can be more assured whether or not you're getting pastured poultry. Look for Amish producers, many of whom follow animal welfare guidelines, or for poultry products with Certified Humane, Animal Welfare Approved, or Animal Welfare Certified stamps.

When I buy poultry, I also tend to source whole birds and cut them (or have the butcher cut them) into pieces for different uses. This minimizes waste and ensures that I'm not serving myself or my husband chicken breast from two different animals. I can also save all the bones after we eat for amazingly comforting, collagen-rich bone broth (see page 57), which is great for immune health and glowing skin!

Roasted Chicken Thighs with Spanish-Style Romesco Sauce and Rice

Prep time: 15 minutes | **Cook time:** 25 to 30 minutes | **Serves** 4

Baking the chicken thighs makes this a go-to recipe for easy weeknight dinners. While traditional Spanish Romesco sauce calls for bread crumbs, I skipped them to make this Pegan friendly, focusing more on the roasted red pepper and rich almond flavor. I like to serve this chicken with Easy Cauliflower Rice (page 107) to soak up the juices from the chicken and the sauce. While the yellow color of Spanish rice traditionally comes from saffron, this one uses turmeric instead for a similar color and savory flavor.

CHICKEN:

8 small bone-in, skin-on chicken thighs
  (about 2 pounds)
1 teaspoon paprika (regular or smoked)
1 teaspoon salt
½ teaspoon freshly ground black pepper
Ground turmeric, as needed
4 cups cooked Easy Cauliflower Rice
  (page 107), warm
Chopped fresh parsley, for garnish

ROMESCO SAUCE:

1 (12-ounce) jar roasted red peppers, drained
½ cup extra-virgin olive oil
½ cup raw almonds
3 tablespoons red wine vinegar
1 clove garlic, smashed
1 teaspoon paprika (regular or smoked)
¼ teaspoon freshly ground black pepper
Pinch salt
Pinch cayenne pepper (optional)

1. Preheat the oven to 475°F.
2. Place the chicken thighs on a roasting pan or in a shallow baking dish. Combine the paprika, salt, and pepper in a small bowl, then rub all over the chicken. Bake until fully cooked through, with an internal temperature of 165°F, 25 to 30 minutes.
3. While the chicken bakes, put the Romesco sauce ingredients into a blender or food processor. Process until smooth and thickened. Set aside, or pour into the jar used for the peppers.

4. Sprinkle turmeric over the warm cauliflower rice and stir to color completely. Spoon about 1 cup of the rice onto each plate. Top with two chicken thighs. Pour the pan juices over all. Spread the Romesco sauce on the chicken pieces (or offer on the side), sprinkle with parsley, and serve.

STORAGE: Save the jar from the roasted peppers to store extra Romesco sauce in the refrigerator for a little over a week, and use to flavor eggs, veggies, and fish. Any extra chicken can be used for quick work-day lunches or dinners for a few days.

INGREDIENT TIP: Turmeric has powerful anti-inflammatory and antioxidant properties. Used in India and East Asia for thousands of years for medicinal purposes, it contains curcumin, which is used for natural pain relief. Even pharmaceutical companies have replicated it in over-the-counter pain relief medication. The curcumin in turmeric is best absorbed when consumed with black pepper and fat; this recipe has both.

PER SERVING: Calories 817; Total fat: 66g; Total carbs: 14g; Fiber: 5g; Sugar: 7g; Protein: 45g; Sodium: 985mg

Gingery Chicken Lettuce Wraps

Prep time: 10 to 15 minutes | **Cook time:** 12 minutes | **Serves** 2 to 4

Inspired by the old-school Thai chicken lettuce wraps I used to enjoy at Asian restaurants, this Pegan-friendly version is heavy on the garlic and ginger for extra flavor. Even if cooking for one or two, I like to make the whole recipe and save leftovers for quick lunches or light dinners. Top with Creamy Citrus Slaw (page 102), if you have any on hand.

1 pound ground chicken

¼ teaspoon salt

¼ teaspoon freshly ground black pepper

3 tablespoons sesame oil, divided

3 tablespoons gluten-free soy sauce, tamari, or coconut aminos, plus more for serving

1 bunch scallions, green and white parts separated

2 tablespoons minced fresh ginger

2 cloves garlic, minced

¼ teaspoon red pepper flakes

1 medium carrot, peeled and cut into ¼-inch dice

3 tablespoons rice vinegar, coconut vinegar, or apple cider vinegar

1 tablespoon water, plus more as needed

1 head butter lettuce

Sesame seeds, for garnish

Chopped fresh cilantro, for garnish

Sriracha or other hot sauce (optional)

Lime wedges (optional)

1. Season the chicken with the salt and pepper.
2. Heat 1 tablespoon of the sesame oil in a large skillet or wok over medium-high heat. When it is hot, add the chicken and cook until browned and cooked through, stirring frequently, 3 to 4 minutes. Using a slotted spoon, transfer the cooked chicken to a bowl. Add the soy sauce and stir to combine.
3. Add 1 tablespoon of the sesame oil and the scallion whites to the pan. Cook, stirring, until the scallions are soft and translucent, about 2 minutes. Add the ginger, garlic, and red pepper flakes and cook until fragrant, 1 minute. Transfer to the bowl with the chicken and toss to combine.
4. Over medium-high heat, add the carrot and vinegar to the pan, which will steam and bubble. Add the water (and more as needed) to cover the carrot dice. Simmer until the carrot is tender and the liquid has evaporated, 3 to 4 minutes. Transfer the mixture to the bowl with the chicken and toss to combine.

5. To serve, separate the head of lettuce into leaves. Top each leaf with the chicken mixture, then add a sprinkling of the scallion greens, sesame seeds, and cilantro. Serve with sriracha and lime wedges, if you like, as well as extra soy sauce.

STORAGE: Store extra scallions wrapped in a damp paper towel in the refrigerator. Leftover cooked chicken will keep for two days in the refrigerator. Cut ginger bulb into smaller chunks and freeze for long-term storage; thaw in the microwave, peel, and chop for use in various dishes.

MAKE IT FASTER: Buy chopped carrot and pre-minced garlic and ginger, if available. You can also use frozen chopped carrots.

PER SERVING: Calories 512; Total fat: 24g; Total carbs: 18g; Fiber: 4g; Sugar: 4g; Protein: 56g; Sodium: 1635mg

Fish & Shellfish

Mussels with Lemon-Garlic-Herb Broth, page 100

Fish and shellfish are an important part of the Pegan diet. Many species come packed with protein; omega-3 fatty acids for brain, heart, and nerve health; and iron, iodine, and other vitamins and minerals. Still, as with grass-fed meat and pastured eggs, it is important to know where your fish comes from and which species to choose, so as to prevent excess mercury and PCB consumption. Ensuring your seafood choices were caught, harvested, or produced in a sustainable way helps protect natural ecosystems that keep your environment—and yourself—as healthy as possible.

Eat Sustainably and Humanely

As the pollution of our waterways increases, it's more important than ever to know our fish sources, not just in order to keep an eye on mercury levels (see Mercury Watch, page 91), but to help lessen our impact on ecosystems. Trying to decide which fish to eat or not eat can be a very confusing endeavor, especially when recommendations change often. Do we eat farmed fish or wild-caught? What is harvested seafood? Has it been harvested sustainably without overharvesting? Are there sustainable sources of farmed fish? Are there mercury issues with some wild-caught ones?

Luckily, there are online resources available such as Monterey Bay Aquarium's Seafood Watch (seafoodwatch.org), which regularly updates its green (good), yellow (fair), and red (poor) seafood choice lists in terms of most to least sustainable. Some farmed shrimp and salmon sources are safe, but you need to know your source. Certain commercial fish farming outlets can cause damage to ocean waters and the environment, which can sicken or even kill wild fish nearby. Alaska has some of the most sustainable wild-caught and harvested fish products on the planet because of strict regulations. Definitely watch out for certain fish products (shrimp, for one) coming from outside the United States, as some countries have come under fire for contributing to ocean destruction, poor food handling, and intentionally mislabeling fish species.

Mercury Watch

From a health perspective, experts recommend eating smaller fish such as sardines, anchovies, and North Atlantic chub mackerel (not King). These species have less mercury because they don't eat other fish, plus they are higher in healthy omega-3 fatty acids. The danger lies in consuming too many larger fish, like tuna, which develop higher mercury levels the bigger they get.

The Natural Resources Defense Council maintains a reputable list of fish sources with the least to highest mercury levels as well as recommended weekly consumption limits. Here are some examples:

Least Mercury Content
(Enjoy frequently)

- Anchovies
- Butterfish
- Catfish
- Clam
- Crab (U.S.)
- Crawfish
- Flounder
- Haddock (Atlantic)
- Hake
- Herring
- Mackerel (North Atlantic)
- Oyster
- Perch (ocean)
- Pollock
- Salmon (canned)
- Salmon (fresh)
- Sardines
- Scallops
- Shrimp
- Sole (Pacific)
- Squid
- Tilapia
- Trout
- Whitefish

Moderate Mercury

(6 or fewer servings per month)

- Bass (striped, black)
- Carp
- Cod (Alaskan)
- Halibut (Atlantic and Pacific)
- Lobster
- Mahi mahi
- Monkfish

- Perch (freshwater)
- Sablefish
- Sea trout
- Skate
- Snapper
- Tuna (canned chunk light)

High Mercury

(3 or fewer servings per month)

- Bluefish
- Chilean sea bass
- Grouper

- Mackerel (Spanish, Gulf of Mexico)
- Tuna, albacore, canned
- Yellowfin tuna

Highest Mercury Content

(Avoid eating)

- King mackerel
- Marlin
- Orange roughy
- Shark

- Swordfish
- Tilefish
- Tuna (bigeye, ahi)

Miso-Glazed Pan-Seared Salmon with Bok Choy

Prep time: 10 minutes | **Cook time:** 10 to 15 minutes | **Serves** 2

2 (6-ounce) salmon fillets

¼ cup white or yellow miso

2 tablespoons rice or coconut vinegar

2 tablespoons sesame oil, divided

1 tablespoon gluten-free soy sauce, tamari, or coconut aminos

1 tablespoon minced fresh ginger

1 clove garlic, minced

1½ pounds (medium bunch) baby bok choy, core removed, sliced into 1½-inch pieces, white stem and leafy green parts separated

2 tablespoons thinly sliced scallion whites (optional)

2 tablespoons thinly sliced scallion greens, for garnish (optional)

1. Heat the broiler to high.
2. On a baking sheet or broiler pan, place the salmon, skin-side down, and pat it dry. In a small bowl, whisk together the miso, vinegar, 1 tablespoon of the sesame oil, the soy sauce, ginger, and garlic. Spread 2 tablespoons of the glaze evenly over the top of the salmon, setting aside the remainder. Let it stand for 10 minutes, if you have time.
3. Broil the salmon until the glaze is bubbly, 3 to 4 minutes. Cover it loosely with foil and continue to broil until slightly pink in the center, another 3 to 4 minutes. Remove the salmon from the broiler, remove the foil, and let it cool.
4. In a large skillet over medium-high heat, heat the remaining 1 tablespoon sesame oil. Add the bok choy stems and scallion whites (if using) and cook until just tender, 2 to 3 minutes. Stir in the remaining miso glaze and cook until fragrant, 30 to 60 seconds. Add the bok choy greens, cover, and steam until just wilted, 30 seconds. Toss to coat with the sauce.
5. To serve, divide the bok choy evenly between two plates. Top each with a salmon fillet and sprinkle with scallion greens (if using).

INGREDIENT TIP: Miso is allowed on the Pegan diet because it is a fermented product, meaning that it's easier to digest. Good bacteria naturally occur in fermented products, which is good for gut health.

MAKE IT FASTER: Marinate salmon with the glaze overnight or up to a few hours before cooking.

PER SERVING: Calories 602; Total fat: 36g; Total carbs: 20g; Fiber: 6g; Sugar: 6g; Protein: 45g; Sodium: 2070mg

Smoked Salmon, Cucumber, and Avocado Sushi

Prep time: 15 minutes | **Serves** 1 to 2

Missing sushi on the Pegan diet? No worries. This easy roll has you covered, and it uses nori sheets, which are now available at many grocery stores. I swapped the rice for creamier, healthier avocado and crunchy cucumber. If you can find wasabi paste and pickled ginger, feel free to use those alongside the extra soy sauce for dipping.

2 sheets sushi nori

1 medium avocado, pitted and peeled

2 tablespoons sesame seeds, divided (optional)

4 ounces smoked salmon (about 4 thin slices)

1 medium cucumber, cut into matchsticks

3 tablespoons pickled ginger (optional)

1 teaspoon wasabi paste (optional)

Gluten-free soy sauce, tamari, or coconut aminos, for dipping

1. Lay 1 piece of nori on a sheet of parchment paper or aluminum foil on a flat surface.
2. In a small bowl, mash the avocado with a fork.
3. Spread half of the avocado mixture on the nori sheet, leaving a ½-inch strip uncovered along the top edge. Sprinkle 1 tablespoon of the sesame seeds (if using), evenly over the avocado. Arrange 2 pieces of the smoked salmon horizontally, covering the avocado.
4. Arrange the cucumber horizontally, running up the length of the sheet and creating columns to cover the salmon.
5. Wet the tip of your finger and run it along the exposed seam. Roll the nori tightly away from you, using the foil as a guide and pressing firmly to seal. Repeat the process with the remaining nori sheet and ingredients, and refrigerate both for at least 30 minutes to firm up.
6. Using a very sharp or serrated knife, slice each roll into 6 to 8 pieces. Serve with pickled ginger and wasabi (if using) and soy sauce for dipping.

STORAGE: Sushi rolls will keep overnight for lunch the next day.

MAKE IT FASTER: Purchase precut cucumber matchsticks or substitute shredded raw slaw. Save extra cucumber matchsticks for Pegan-Style Bibimbap (page 72).

PER SERVING: Calories 487; Total fat: 32g; Total carbs: 26g; Fiber: 15g; Sugar: 6g; Protein: 28g; Sodium: 1976mg

Oil-Poached Whitefish with Lemony Gremolata

Prep time: 1 hour (for marinating), plus 10 minutes | **Cook time:** 15 to 20 minutes | **Serves** 4

This recipe calls for a quick marinade and an oil-based poach in the oven using just one dish for a super simple and quick, delicious meal. I like to marinate the fish in the oil and gremolata for about a half hour while doing other things in the kitchen or braising greens. Then, I just take the fish out of the refrigerator and place it on the countertop until it's room temperature and then pop it in the oven. Cooking fish at this lower temperature (preferably in a glass or ceramic baking dish, not steel), helps prevent drying out the fish. It's best to have the skin removed by the fishmonger or do it yourself, to prevent it from getting rubbery during cooking. Save the lemon used for the zest to cut into wedges for serving.

2 (¾-pound) skinless Arctic char or other whitefish fillets

1 teaspoon kosher salt

1 teaspoon freshly ground black pepper

½ cup extra-virgin olive oil

3 cloves garlic, minced

¾ cup fresh parsley leaves, minced, divided

¼ cup grated lemon zest (from 6 small or 4 large lemons), divided

1. Place the fish fillets lengthwise in a 13-by-9-inch baking dish and season with the salt and pepper on both sides. In a small bowl, whisk together the olive oil, garlic, half of the parsley, and half of the lemon zest. Pour evenly over the fish, cover, and marinate in the refrigerator for at least 30 minutes and up to overnight.
2. Preheat the oven to 350°F.
3. Bake the fish until just cooked through, 15 to 20 minutes. Cut each fillet into 2 pieces, top evenly with the remaining parsley and lemon zest, and serve with Lemony Sautéed Chard with Red Onion and Herbs (page 109) or another vegetable side or salad.

PER SERVING: Calories 535; Total fat: 28g; Total carbs: 3g; Fiber: 1g; Sugar: 1g; Protein: 37g; Sodium: 622mg

Ceviche Fish Tacos with Easy Guacamole

Prep time: 15 minutes plus 4 to 6 hours for marinating | **Serves** 4

Some days you just don't feel like cooking. That's where ceviche comes in handy, especially on warm-weather days. Make the ceviche earlier in the day for a quick-and-easy, hands-off lunch or dinner. The citrus juices cook the fish over several hours, so it's safe to eat. But, if you would rather not eat fish that is technically raw, feel free to use precooked shrimp for the recipe.

CEVICHE:

1¼ pounds meaty skinless fresh fish fillets (wild-caught or Hamachi tuna, halibut, tilapia, barramundi, or mahi mahi), cut into ½-inch cubes

3 tablespoons lime juice

3 tablespoons lemon juice

¼ teaspoon salt

¼ teaspoon freshly ground black pepper

2 ripe plum or heirloom tomatoes, seeded and chopped (juices reserved)

1 tablespoon olive oil

¾ cup chopped red onion

1 serrano pepper, seeded and minced (optional)

Bibb lettuce leaves, for serving

GUACAMOLE:

4 avocados

Juice from ½ lime (reserve remaining half for wedges, for serving)

½ cup chopped fresh cilantro

2 tablespoons chopped red onion

1 serrano pepper, seeded and minced

ADDITIONAL TACO FIXINGS:

Store-bought salsa (without added salt, oil, or sugar)

Creamy Citrus Slaw (page 102)

Chopped fresh cilantro

Lime wedges

Quick-Pickled Red Onions (page 115)

1. In a medium bowl, place the fish, lime and lemon juices, salt, and pepper and toss to combine. Cover tightly and chill until the fish turns completely white, tossing occasionally, at least 4 hours and up to 6 hours.

2. Meanwhile, make the guacamole. Cut the avocados in half, then remove the pit and peel. Spoon the avocado into a large bowl and mash it with a large metal spoon. Add the lime juice and continue to mix and mash until mostly smooth with some remaining chunks (this helps prevent the guacamole from browning). Mix in the cilantro, onion, and serrano pepper. Cover tightly and refrigerate until ready to use.

3. Strain the fish, moving it to a clean bowl; discard the marinade. Add the tomatoes, oil, onion, and serrano pepper (if using) and toss gently to combine. Serve wrapped in the Bibb lettuce leaves topped with the guacamole and your choice of additional fixings.

STORAGE: Eat ceviche the day you make it, and the sooner the better; at a certain point the citrus juice compromises the fish's texture and makes it mushy. Store extra guacamole with plastic wrap laid right on top of it to prevent browning.

PER SERVING: Calories 509; Total fat: 31g; Total carbs: 31g; Fiber: 13g; Sugar: 3g; Protein: 43g; Sodium: 121mg

Shrimp Scampi with Baby Spinach

Prep time: 5 minutes | **Cook time:** 10 minutes | **Serves** 2 to 4

Traditional scampi recipes call for langoustine and leave the shells on, but large or medium-sized peeled shrimp works just as well for this quick-and-easy dinner (or luxurious lunch!). Leaving the shells on helps develop more flavor. By swapping the usual bread crumbs or flour for extra garlic, it's also Pegan friendly, and tasty.

1 pound jumbo shrimp (about 12), peeled and deveined

3 tablespoons extra-virgin olive oil, divided

6 cloves garlic, minced

1 cup unsalted chicken broth or stock

Grated zest and juice from 1 medium lemon

½ teaspoon red pepper flakes, or to taste

¼ teaspoon sea salt or Himalayan salt, or to taste

½ teaspoon freshly ground black pepper, or to taste

¼ cup (½ stick) cold unsalted grass-fed butter, cubed

6 to 8 cups (6 ounces) baby spinach leaves

2 to 3 tablespoons chopped fresh parsley (optional)

1. Pat the shrimp very dry with paper towels. Heat 2 tablespoons of the olive oil in a large skillet over medium-high heat. Add the shrimp and cook until pink, flipping once, about 2 minutes per side. Transfer to a large bowl or plate.

2. Reduce the heat to medium and add remaining 1 tablespoon oil. Add the garlic and cook until just fragrant, about 1 minute. Add the broth, lemon zest and juice, red pepper flakes, salt, and black pepper, increase the heat to medium-high, and bring to a simmer. Reduce the sauce by half, scraping up any browned bits from the bottom with a wooden spoon, about 5 minutes.

3. Remove the pan from the heat and allow to cool slightly. Add butter, one cube at a time, stirring continually with a wooden spoon until the sauce thickens.

4. To serve, divide spinach evenly among four plates. Top each plate with about 4 shrimp. Divide the sauce evenly among the plates and garnish with the parsley (if using).

INGREDIENT TIP: Keep the butter chilled in the refrigerator until just ready to use.

VARIATIONS: Serve with zucchini noodles (page 101), spaghetti squash (page 74), or quinoa.

PER SERVING: Calories 644; Total fat: 46g; Total carbs: 9g; Fiber: 2g; Sugar: 3g; Protein: 53g; Sodium: 826mg

Shrimp Fried Rice

Prep time: 15 minutes | **Cook time:** 20 to 25 minutes | **Serves** 4

While this dish is often served as a side for takeout, this is more of a main course for an easy, light, and satisfying dinner.

3 tablespoons gluten-free soy sauce, tamari, or coconut aminos

2 tablespoons minced fresh ginger

3 tablespoons sesame oil, divided

2 large eggs, lightly beaten

⅔ to ¾ pound medium shrimp, peeled and deveined (about 24)

1 shallot, minced

1 red bell pepper, seeded and diced

1 recipe cooled or chilled Easy Cauliflower Rice (page 107)

¾ cup frozen peas

¼ cup chopped unsalted cashews

2 tablespoons chopped fresh cilantro

¼ teaspoon red pepper flakes (optional)

Sliced scallion greens, for garnish (optional)

1. In a small bowl, whisk the soy sauce and ginger together and set aside.

2. In a wok or large skillet over medium heat, heat 1 tablespoon of the sesame oil. Add the eggs and cook, stirring frequently with a wooden spoon or spatula, until scrambled. Transfer to a small bowl and break up the cooked egg into small pieces using two forks. Set aside.

3. In the same wok over medium-high heat, heat 1 tablespoon of the sesame oil. Add the shrimp and cook, tossing, until bright pink but not browned, 3 to 4 minutes. Transfer the shrimp to a separate plate or bowl and set aside.

4. Add the remaining 1 tablespoon sesame oil and the shallot to the wok and cook until fragrant, tossing frequently, about 30 seconds. Add the bell pepper and cook until just tender, tossing occasionally, about 2 minutes. Add the cauliflower rice and cook, tossing occasionally, until lightly browned and crisp, about 5 minutes. Stir in the soy sauce mixture. Add the cooked shrimp, cooked eggs, and peas and stir until well combined and heated through, 2 to 3 minutes. Add the cashews, cilantro, and red pepper flakes (if using), tossing to combine.

5. Divide the mixture among four bowls, garnish with scallion greens (if using) and serve.

> **MAKE IT FASTER:** Purchase precooked cauliflower rice (thaw completely if frozen). Purchase chopped bell pepper, if available.

PER SERVING: Calories 335; Total fat: 18g; Total carbs: 18g; Fiber: 5g; Sugar: 6g; Protein: 27g; Sodium: 957mg

Mussels with Lemon-Garlic-Herb Broth

Prep time: 10 minutes | **Cook time:** 8 minutes | **Serves** 4

Mussels are one of the more inexpensive seafood items you can buy, and they are super Pegan friendly, low in mercury, and sustainably harvested. Plus, they only take a few minutes to cook, which makes for an easy weeknight meal. It's up to you if you want to stir the spinach into the broth for added nutrition, or pair this recipe with any vegetable side dishes in this book.

2 pounds mussels

1 tablespoon extra-virgin olive oil

2 shallots, minced

3 cloves garlic, minced

2 cups chicken or Veggie Trimmings Stock (page 61)

¼ cup lemon juice (from 2 lemons)

¼ cup chopped fresh parsley, plus more for garnish

¼ cup chopped fresh dill (optional)

3 tablespoons chopped fresh thyme

½ teaspoon salt

¼ teaspoon freshly ground black pepper

¼ teaspoon red pepper flakes (optional)

3 cups baby spinach (or spinach leaves torn into smaller pieces)

2 tablespoons cold unsalted grass-fed butter, cubed

1. Rinse the mussels under cold running water, pulling off their black beards as needed. Place in a strainer to drain and set aside.

2. Heat the oil in a large, deep skillet, stockpot, or Dutch oven over medium-high heat. Add the shallots and cook, stirring, until soft and translucent, about 2 minutes. Add the garlic and cook until fragrant, 30 seconds. Add the stock, lemon juice, herbs, salt, pepper, and red pepper flakes (if using), stirring to combine. Bring the stock to a boil.

3. Add the mussels, cover, and cook, undisturbed, until the mussels open their shells, about 5 minutes. Reduce the heat to low. Discard any mussels that have not yet opened. Divide the mussels among four large serving bowls.

4. Add the spinach to the broth, cover, and cook until just wilted, 1 to 2 minutes. Remove the lid and turn off the heat. Let sit for 1 minute, then add the cold butter, one piece at a time, stirring in each one until fully melted before adding the next one.

5. Spoon the broth over the mussels in the bowls, garnish with more parsley if you like, and serve.

PER SERVING: Calories 342; Total fat: 16g; Total carbs: 17g; Fiber: 2g; Sugar: 2g; Protein: 31g; Sodium: 653mg

Clam Linguine with Zucchini Noodles

Prep time: 10 minutes | **Cook time:** 20 minutes | **Serves** 4

For this easy and delicious weeknight meal, feel free to step things up with fresh clams and bottled clam juice, if desired. High-quality canned clams and their juices work great, too, and when combined with a hearty portion of grass-fed butter, you can't go wrong. Feel free to use spaghetti squash strands (see page 74) in place of the zucchini noodles, if you have those on hand or prefer a richer taste. To ensure the sauce doesn't break, keep the cubed butter in the refrigerator until just before use.

2 medium zucchini

2 tablespoons extra-virgin olive oil

4 cloves garlic, minced

4 (6-ounce) cans chopped clams

½ teaspoon red pepper flakes

¼ cup (½ stick) cold unsalted grass-fed butter, cubed

2 teaspoons grated lemon zest

Chopped fresh parsley, for garnish

Freshly ground black pepper

2 lemon wedges, for garnish (optional)

1. Using a spiralizer, cut the zucchini into noodles or use purchased zoodles (thaw if frozen). Set aside.

2. In a large, deep skillet over medium-high heat, heat olive oil and garlic until fragrant, 1 to 2 minutes, taking care that the garlic doesn't brown. Drain the liquid from clams into the skillet, leaving the clams in the cans. Add the red pepper flakes. Bring to a simmer and cook until the liquid is reduced to ¾ cup, about 15 minutes.

3. Add the clams to the broth and cook until heated through, about 1 minute. Turn off the heat and let sit for 1 minute.

4. Add the butter, stirring in each cube until fully melted before adding the next one. Stir in the lemon zest. Add zucchini noodles and toss to coat.

5. To serve, divide between four plates or shallow bowls. Top with parsley and black pepper, and serve with lemon wedges, if desired.

MAKE IT FASTER: Purchase premade fresh or frozen zucchini noodles (zoodles).

VARIATIONS: Swap the canned clams with 1 cup jarred clam juice and 2 pounds fresh clams. Cover and cook until they open, 5 to 8 minutes.

PER SERVING: Calories 333; Total fat: 20g; Total carbs: 7g; Fiber: 1g; Sugar: 2g; Protein: 22g; Sodium: 231mg

Crab Cakes with Creamy Citrus Slaw

Prep time: 10 minutes | **Cook time:** 7 minutes | **Serves** 2

I love these crab cakes because they showcase the crab, Maryland style, rather than using bread crumbs and other fillers like those tasteless hockey-puck versions. Instead, this recipe calls for a touch of mashed Easy Cauliflower Rice (set some aside next time you make it, just for this use) and eggs as binder. Feel free to substitute the crab with canned tuna, which can cost less, but check the label to make sure it's line-caught albacore packed in water, which is lower in mercury than other varieties. There are more domestic companies sourcing sustainable, low-mercury tuna these days.

SLAW:

1 (14-ounce) package shredded coleslaw mix

Grated zest and juice of 1 medium lemon

Grated zest of 1 medium navel orange

2 tablespoons Dijon mustard

CRAB CAKES:

2 large eggs

1 tablespoon Dijon mustard

½ teaspoon sea salt

½ teaspoon Old Bay seasoning or paprika

¼ teaspoon freshly ground black pepper

1 (16-ounce) can cooked jumbo lump crab meat, drained and patted dry

¾ cup cooled or chilled cooked Easy Cauliflower Rice (page 107), mashed with a fork

2 tablespoons chopped fresh parsley

2 tablespoons extra-virgin olive oil

1. To make the slaw, toss the coleslaw mix with the lemon zest and juice, orange zest, and mustard in a large bowl until evenly coated. Refrigerate for at least 30 minutes.

2. In a medium bowl, whisk together the eggs, mustard, salt, Old Bay seasoning, and pepper. Fold in the crab, cauliflower rice, and parsley until well combined. Refrigerate until slightly firm, about 10 minutes.

3. Remove the crab mixture from the refrigerator and form into four patties about 2 inches thick and 3 inches in diameter.

4. Heat the olive oil in a large skillet or cast iron pan over medium-high heat. When the oil is hot, add two of the crab cakes. Cook until golden brown, about 3 minutes per side. Transfer to a paper towel–lined plate. Repeat with the remaining cakes.

5. Place two crab cakes on each plate and serve with the chilled slaw.

STORAGE: Slaw will keep in an airtight container in the refrigerator for three days.

PER SERVING: Calories 438; Total fat: 21g; Total carbs: 15g; Fiber: 7g; Sugar: 7g; Protein: 52g; Sodium: 1134mg

CHAPTER 8

Easy Sides

Garlicky Green Beans, page 108

These easy, vegetable-rich recipes can be paired with Pegan-friendly proteins, or even other vegetable sides, for a complete meal. Most are pretty simple to make and can even be made ahead of time. Note that greens are always best cooked fresh, but you can make the coconut rice, carrots, mushrooms, roasted squash, cauliflower rice, and ratatouille in batches a day or two before you plan to eat them. Ratatouille and coconut rice, in particular, freeze well for longer term storage and quick-and-easy reheated lunches and dinners. I have also included a recipe for Quick-Pickled Red Onions (page 115), which is more of a garnish or topping. So simple to make and store, these onions add just the right amount of brightness, acidity, and crunch to just about any dish, from Pegan "tacos" and wraps to salads and fish dishes.

Easy Cauliflower Rice

Prep time: 5 minutes | **Cook time:** 5 to 8 minutes | **Serves** 4 (makes 4 cups)

You can pair cauliflower rice with just about anything. This versatile, Pegan-friendly side can be used in place of traditional rice for stir-fries and as a bed for any protein or veggie. The coconut oil helps tone down the unpleasant aroma that can sometimes occur when cooking cauliflower, but you can substitute olive oil if you prefer.

1 head fresh cauliflower, greens
  removed, washed
1 tablespoon coconut oil or extra-virgin
  olive oil
Salt, to taste
Freshly ground black pepper, to taste

1. Break the cauliflower into florets, put in a food processor, and pulse in 1-second intervals 10 to 15 times, until the cauliflower resembles rice. Alternately, grate the florets using the medium-size slots of a box grater.

2. Heat the coconut oil in a large skillet over medium heat until melted. Add the cauliflower, cover, and cook until softened and the odor dissipates, 5 to 8 minutes.

3. Remove the lid, season with salt and pepper, and fluff with a fork.

MAKE IT FASTER: Look for cauliflower rice in the frozen vegetable aisle of your favorite grocery store, as many stores now carry this product. Freeze any extra cooked or uncooked cauliflower rice for up to 2 months. You can also microwave the cauliflower in a glass or porcelain bowl, covered, for 3 minutes. Carefully remove the lid and fluff with a fork. Cauliflower rice will last in the refrigerator for 5 days.

PER SERVING: Calories 82; Total fat: 4g; Total carbs: 11g; Fiber: 5g; Sugar: 5g; Protein: 4g; Sodium: 63mg

Garlicky Green Beans

Prep time: 5 minutes | **Cook time:** 7 minutes | **Serves** 2 to 4

This is a super easy recipe that is very flavorful and nutritious, as garlic—and green beans, for that matter—is loaded with antioxidants. Cooking the garlic for a longer time in the oil essentially creates a flavored oil with crispy, toasted garlic pieces to coat the green beans. A little extra water on the green beans after washing helps them steam faster.

¾ to 1 pound green beans

3 tablespoons extra-virgin olive oil

3 cloves garlic, minced

¼ teaspoon sea salt or Himalayan salt

¼ teaspoon freshly ground black pepper, or to taste

Chopped or sliced almonds, for garnish

1. Trim the ends of the green beans by snapping them off by hand or by slicing multiple beans at once with a knife. Give them a quick rinse and set aside.
2. In a large skillet over medium heat, heat the olive oil. When it is hot, add the garlic and cook, stirring frequently, until lightly browned and very fragrant, 1 to 2 minutes. Add the green beans, tossing to coat with the oil. Cover and cook until the beans are tender, 4 to 5 minutes.
3. Season the beans with the salt and pepper, giving them a quick toss.
4. Transfer the green beans to a plate or bowl, scraping the garlic from the pan over the beans. Garnish with almonds (if using) and serve.

> **MAKE IT FASTER:** Purchase minced garlic and trimmed green beans, if available.

PER SERVING: Calories 258; Total fat: 21g; Total carbs: 18g; Fiber: 8g; Sugar: 3g; Protein: 5g; Sodium: 249mg

Lemony Sautéed Chard with Red Onion and Herbs

Prep time: 5 minutes | **Cook time:** 5 to 7 minutes | **Serves** 2 to 4

Enjoy this easy side dish by itself, with some chopped almonds for crunch, or as a bed for just about any protein, including a 30-Second Egg (page 45). Topping off this side dish with fresh herbs adds an extra dose of flavor, crunch, and nutrition. Feel free to add garlic after cooking the onions and stems. Serve the greens with lemon juice squeezed on top; adding lemon juice during the cooking can brown the greens.

1 large bunch (1 pound) Swiss or
    rainbow chard

1 large lemon

2 tablespoons extra-virgin olive oil

½ medium red onion, minced

¼ teaspoon salt

¼ teaspoon freshly ground black pepper

Leaves from 1 small bunch fresh herbs
    (parsley, cilantro, basil, or dill), minced
    (optional)

1. Rinse and lightly pat dry the chard (a little water helps them steam faster). Slice the stems into ½-inch pieces and set aside. Tear the leafy greens into 3-inch pieces and set aside.

2. Using a zester or the fine side of a box grater, grate the lemon and set the zest aside. Cut the lemon into wedges and set aside.

3. Heat the olive oil in a large skillet or Dutch oven over medium heat. When it is hot, add onion and chard stems and cook, stirring occasionally, until soft and translucent, 2 to 4 minutes. Add the greens, cover, and steam until just wilted, about 1 minute. Remove the lid, add the reserved lemon zest, salt, pepper, and herbs (if using). Toss to combine.

4. Serve the greens with the lemon wedges for squeezing just before enjoying.

> **MAKE IT FASTER:** Purchase minced garlic, if available.

PER SERVING: Calories 176; Total fat: 15g; Total carbs: 11g; Fiber: 4g; Sugar: 4g; Protein: 4g; Sodium: 777mg

Perfectly Sautéed Mushrooms with Rosemary and Baby Greens

Prep time: 5 minutes | **Cook time:** 15 minutes | **Serves** 2 to 4

Rosemary brings out the savory flavor of the mushrooms in this recipe. Plus, did you know this herb is a nutritional powerhouse? Rosemary contains everything from iron and potassium to fiber, copper, calcium, magnesium, B vitamins, and folates. Strip off the needles by holding the stem with one hand and pinching the needles in a downward fashion with your other thumb and forefinger.

10 ounces cremini or baby portabella mushrooms

2 tablespoons extra-virgin olive oil

¼ teaspoon salt

¼ teaspoon freshly ground black pepper

4 cups baby greens (spinach, kale, or a mix)

1 tablespoon chopped fresh rosemary

1. Clean any dirt off of the mushrooms with a paper towel. Cut the mushrooms into ½-inch-thick slices.

2. Heat the olive oil in a large skillet over medium-high heat. When it is hot, add the mushrooms in a single layer and cook, not stirring or flipping, until browned on one side, about 2 minutes. Flip the mushrooms and cook until browned on the other side, about 2 minutes. Reduce the heat to medium and continue to cook until the mushrooms have released their juices and are tender, another 5 to 8 minutes. Season with the salt and pepper.

3. Add the baby greens, cover, and cook until just wilted, 30 to 60 seconds. Stir in the rosemary and serve.

PER SERVING: Calories 178; Total fat: 15g; Total carbs: 9g; Fiber: 3g; Sugar: 3g; Protein: 5g; Sodium: 348mg

Maple-Roasted Delicata Squash with Hazelnuts

Prep time: 10 minutes | **Cook time:** 40 minutes | **Serves** 2 to 4

Delicata squash—the long, thick hot dog–shaped squash with green zebra stripes—is a great squash to eat. Unlike butternut and, in some cases, acorn squash, the delicata squash skin softens and becomes edible once roasted. Plus, enjoying the skin helps increase your fiber intake. Only a touch of maple syrup is necessary to bring out the naturally sweet flavors of the squash. Hazelnuts are optional, but they add a nice flavor and crunch.

2 medium delicata squash (about 2 pounds)

1 tablespoon extra-virgin olive oil

1 tablespoon maple syrup

¼ teaspoon salt

¼ teaspoon freshly ground black pepper

¼ cup chopped lightly toasted hazelnuts (optional)

1. Preheat the oven to 425°F.
2. Slice each squash lengthwise in half. Scoop out the seeds. Flip the squash, cut-side down, and slice into 1-inch pieces.
3. Place the squash on a baking sheet and toss with the olive oil and maple syrup until evenly coated. Spread out the squash in a single layer so the pieces do not overlap. Roast until tender and browned, flipping once halfway, 20 to 25 minutes.
4. Season with the salt and pepper, then sprinkle with the hazelnuts (if using), and serve.

PER SERVING: Calories 247; Total fat: 7g; Total carbs: 41g; Fiber: 5g; Sugar: 22g; Protein: 5g; Sodium: 292mg

Paprika-Dusted Sweet Potato Fries

Prep time: 20 minutes | **Cook time:** 20 minutes | **Serves** 2 to 4

No need to miss French fries on the Pegan diet with this far more nutritious and satisfying substitution. Adding a pinch of regular or smoked paprika adds a little extra umami to balance out the sweetness of the potatoes. If you don't have paprika or want to use another spice, try chili powder, cumin, or a pinch of cayenne for heat. Fresh dill gives the fries a nice look and a bright, herby taste, but is totally optional.

2 large sweet potatoes (¾ pound total), peeled

1 tablespoon extra-virgin olive oil or melted coconut oil

½ teaspoon salt

¼ teaspoon freshly ground black pepper

½ teaspoon paprika (regular or smoked)

3 tablespoons chopped fresh dill (optional)

1. Preheat the oven to 425°F. Line a baking sheet with aluminum foil or parchment paper.
2. Slice the sweet potatoes lengthwise in half and then into ¼-by-¼-inch matchsticks, adding them to a large bowl of cold water to soak for a few minutes while prepping (soaking helps remove excess starch so they crisp up after baking). Drain and dry thoroughly with paper towels.
3. Place the potatoes on the prepared baking sheet. Toss with the oil and spread out in a single layer so the fries are not overlapping or touching. Turn all the pieces to point in the same direction.
4. Bake for 15 minutes, remove from the oven, and flip the fries using a flat metal spatula. Make sure the fries are not overlapping or touching and are facing the same direction.
5. Return to the oven and bake until the fries are browned and cooked through, another 15 minutes. Turn off the oven, prop open the door, and allow the fries to cool and crisp up for 10 minutes.
6. Remove from the oven and season with the salt, pepper, and paprika (if using). Toss to coat, sprinkle with the dill (if using), and enjoy.

MAKE IT FASTER: Purchase precut sweet potatoes from the freezer aisle, if available.

PER SERVING: Calories 261; Total fat: 7g; Total carbs: 48g; Fiber: 7g; Sugar: 1g; Protein: 3g; Sodium: 597mg

Coconut-Glazed Carrots

Prep time: 3 minutes | **Cook time:** 15 minutes | **Serves** 4

This is a simple go-to recipe for a hearty vegetable side. While cooked carrots are slightly higher on the glycemic index than raw, the healthy fat from the coconut oil helps balance out the dish in flavor and nutrition.

1 pound carrots, peeled

3 tablespoons coconut oil

¼ teaspoon salt

¼ teaspoon freshly ground black pepper

1 cup full-fat coconut milk or water

1. Slice the carrots at an angle into 2½-inch pieces.

2. Heat the coconut oil in a large Dutch oven or skillet over medium heat. Add the carrots and turn to coat; season with the salt and pepper. Pour in the coconut milk and bring to a boil. Reduce the heat to a simmer, cover, and cook until the carrots are just tender, 7 to 10 minutes.

3. Remove the lid, increase the heat, and continue to cook until the water fully evaporates, then serve.

STORAGE: Leftovers will keep in the refrigerator for three days; freeze for up to two months.

VARIATIONS: Season the carrots with any additional spice you desire once the water has evaporated and immediately before serving: turmeric, curry powder, cumin, regular or smoked paprika, chili powder, cayenne pepper, or onion or garlic powder. Even cinnamon and nutmeg will work.

PER SERVING: Calories 273; Total fat: 25g; Total carbs: 15g; Fiber: 4g; Sugar: 8g; Protein: 2g; Sodium: 234mg

Garden Ratatouille

Prep time: 10 minutes | **Cook time:** 20 minutes | **Serves** 4

Ratatouille is a great way to use up veggies in your kitchen, especially during peak harvest in the summer, and it freezes well. It's also a very versatile side dish that can be served over spaghetti squash as a meat-free main course or spread on cucumber rounds for a bruschetta-like appetizer. Served cold, ratatouille is simply great for snacking, too. Enjoy!

2 tablespoons extra-virgin olive oil

1 small onion, chopped

1 small eggplant, unpeeled, cut into ½-inch cubes

1 large red bell pepper, seeded and cut into ½-inch pieces

1 large zucchini, cut into ½-inch cubes

6 to 8 ripe tomatoes, cut into ½-inch pieces, reserving the juices

¼ cup packed fresh basil leaves, chopped

¼ teaspoon salt

¼ teaspoon freshly ground black pepper

1. Heat the olive oil in a large, deep skillet or Dutch oven over medium heat. Add the onion and eggplant and cook, stirring occasionally, until the onion is slightly browned and the eggplant is tender, about 5 minutes.

2. Add the bell pepper and zucchini and cook, stirring occasionally, until tender, about 10 minutes. Stir in the tomatoes and their juices, cover, and simmer until the vegetables are tender and the ratatouille thickens, 5 minutes.

3. Remove the lid, stir in the basil, and season with the salt and pepper. Serve warm or cover and chill for at least 1 hour or up to overnight to serve cold; this allows the flavors to meld.

STORAGE: Ratatouille will keep in the refrigerator for up to 4 days and in the freezer for up to 2 months.

MAKE IT FASTER: You may make this dish the day or night before. Just chill it and serve cold the next day or two.

VARIATIONS: Feel free to omit certain vegetables (except for the tomatoes) from the list. You may substitute 2 cups of diced or crushed tomatoes (without any sugar or salt added) for the fresh tomatoes if they're not in season.

PER SERVING: Calories 163; Total fat: 8g; Total carbs: 23g; Fiber: 9g; Sugar: 14g; Protein: 5g; Sodium: 171mg

Quick-Pickled Red Onions

Prep Time: 5 minutes | **Makes** about 2 cups onions

Raw red onions can be a little sharp for me, so I enjoy this pickled version atop all sorts of dishes like tacos, salads, and fish for a little extra acid and sweetness to balance other flavors. This method of pickling is super easy and only takes time, not heat. Feel free to continue adding more diced onion to the jar with the vinegar over the course of 2 to 3 weeks, removing onions from the jar as needed, using a fork or slotted spoon.

1 large red onion, diced into ½-inch pieces

2 cups apple cider vinegar

1 teaspoon salt

1 tablespoon whole black peppercorns

1. In a large glass jar or bowl with a lid, add the onions, vinegar, salt, and pepper. Give the mixture a quick stir.
2. Cover and refrigerate overnight. The onions will keep in the refrigerator for about 3 weeks.

PER SERVING (¼ CUP): Calories 22; Total fat: 0g; Total carbs: 3g; Fiber: 1g; Sugar: 1g; Protein: 0g; Sodium: 295mg

CHAPTER 9

Snacks & Sweets

Coconut-Banana Ice Cream, page 122

Snacks and sweets don't have to be off-limits on the Pegan diet. In fact, using nuts in multiple forms (chopped, as butter or milk, coconut oil), low-GI fruit, and touches of pure maple syrup and raw honey here and there will add richness and nutrition, even if you're technically "indulging." Don't forget to cut up and freeze some of these sweet treats like the lemon tart and truffles for on-demand dessert. The snack ideas in this chapter are dairy-free and sugar-free as well as delicious, and will keep you fueled between meals. I like to make batches of the dips, crackers, and apple chips on the weekend to enjoy, not only as a satisfying snack, but as a super light lunch on less ravenous days. They also travel well for light meals and bites on the go.

Vegan Cream Cheese Dip

Prep time: 8 minutes, plus 1 hour for soaking | **Serves** 2 to 4 (makes about 1 cup)

Cashews are most nutritious in raw form, but they can be hard to digest when eaten that way. Soaking them for at least an hour is the best way to break them down. Use this dip in place of mayonnaise in dressings and aioli. It can also substitute for cream in soups and sweets; just add more water, 1 tablespoon at a time, to the base recipe.

1 cup raw cashews

2 teaspoons lemon juice

¼ teaspoon salt

¼ teaspoon freshly ground black pepper

3 tablespoons cold water, plus more as needed

1. Soak the cashews in a bowl of water to cover for at least 1 hour and up to overnight in the refrigerator. Drain, briefly rinse, and transfer the cashews to a food processor. Add the lemon juice, salt, and pepper and pulse until combined, about 1 minute.

2. Scrape down the sides of the food processor with a rubber spatula, add the water, and process until smooth, 2 to 4 minutes, adding more water by the teaspoon to thin it out if needed. Add optional dip flavors (see Customize Your Dip) and process until combined.

3. Serve with Gluten-Free Seedy Crackers (page 120) or crudités such as celery, cucumber, and bell pepper strips.

> **STORAGE:** Store the cream cheese dip in a jar or other airtight container in the refrigerator for about a week.

PER SERVING: Calories 351; Total fat: 26g; Total carbs: 17g; Fiber: 2g; Sugar: 0g; Protein: 11g; Sodium: 298mg

Customize Your Dip

It's so easy to change up this dip to suit your taste; just add these ingredients to the food processor along with the cashews:

RED PEPPER AND GARLIC: 1 quarter of a roasted red bell pepper (from a jar, drained) and 1 teaspoon garlic powder.

ONION AND CHIVE: 1 tablespoon onion powder. Garnish with caramelized onions and minced fresh chives.

SESAME: 1 tablespoon sesame oil. Garnish with toasted sesame seeds.

SPICY AND SAVORY: 1 tablespoon nutritional yeast and 2 teaspoons chili powder, or to taste.

Gluten-Free Seedy Crackers

Prep time: 10 minutes | **Cook time:** 30 minutes | **Serves** 6

These grain-free, seed-based crackers are a must for the pegan diet; they satisfy cravings for crunch and make the perfect vehicle for pegan-friendly dips, spreads, and nut butters. Crush up a bunch as a topper for soups and salads, or throw some in your work bag for a quick, healthy, fat-fueled bite on the go. These crackers take a little bit of time to make, so I like to make batches on the weekend for noshing during the week.

¾ cup sesame seeds

⅓ cup sunflower seeds

¼ cup chia seeds

3 tablespoons pepitas (pumpkin seeds)

2 tablespoons flaxseeds

1⅔ cups water

1 teaspoon salt

3 tablespoons coconut oil, melted

1. Preheat the oven to 350°F.
2. In a large bowl, combine the seeds with the water and let them soak until they have absorbed the liquid and a thick dough forms, about 20 minutes.
3. Add the salt and stir well to combine.
4. Lightly grease a baking sheet with 1 tablespoon of the melted coconut oil.
5. Using a rubber spatula or wooden spoon, spread the dough in a thin layer (¼ inch or less) on the baking sheet. Brush the top with the remaining 2 tablespoons coconut oil and bake until set and slightly browned on one side, about 1 hour.
6. Remove the baking sheet from the oven. When cool enough to handle, carefully break the cracker into smaller pieces.

STORAGE: Crackers will keep in an airtight container for about a week; freeze for up to 2 months.

PER SERVING: Calories 262; Total fat: 23g; Total carbs: 10g; Fiber: 6g; Sugar: 0g; Protein: 7g; Sodium: 393mg

Spiced Apple Chips

Prep time: 5 to 7 minutes | **Cook time:** 2 hours | **Serves** 4 (makes about 3 cups)

Move over, carb-ridden potato chips. This crunchy snack has the best of both worlds: natural sweetness (but not too much) from the apple and a touch of salt for balance. Feel free to play around with various spices listed here. These go great with a little spread of nut butter for an afternoon snack.

2 apples, cored

¼ teaspoon salt

1. Preheat the oven to 275°F. Line a baking sheet with aluminum foil or parchment paper.
2. Using a mandoline or sharp knife, thinly slice the apples. Spread them out flat on the prepared baking sheet in an even layer. Sprinkle evenly with the salt and, if desired, other spices (see Spice It Up, right).
3. Bake until crisp on one side, about 1 hour. Turn the slices over and bake until completely crisped and lightly browned, another hour.
4. Remove from the oven and allow to cool before storing.

STORAGE: Store chips in an airtight container at room temperature for up to 1 week.

VARIATION: To make kale chips, tear the leaves off the ribs of 1 bunch of kale and into 1½-inch pieces, massage the leaves with 2 tablespoons olive oil, spread out on a baking sheet in an even layer, and roast at 275°F until crisp, turning the leaves once, about 20 minutes.

PER SERVING: Calories 58; Total fat: 0g; Total carbs: 15g; Fiber: 3g; Sugar: 11g; Protein: 0g; Sodium: 148mg

Spice It Up

These chips take well to a host of different flavors. Here are five of my favorites; toss them with the apples to coat evenly before baking:

CINNAMON: 2 teaspoons ground cinnamon, or to taste

SPICY: 2 teaspoons chili powder, or to taste

SMOKY: 2 teaspoons smoked paprika or chipotle powder, or to taste

PUMPKIN SPICE: ¼ teaspoon each ground cinnamon, ginger, nutmeg, and cloves

Coconut-Banana Ice Cream

Prep time: 4 minutes, plus an hour to freeze the bananas | **Serves** 2 to 4 (makes 2 cups)

This recipe was inspired by The Endless Meal blog and requires a strong food processor or blender. After you try this Pegan-friendly ice cream, you'll no longer want the sugary dairy stuff that can cause stomachaches and weight gain, anyway. I recommend peeling and cutting the bananas into small, even chunks before freezing them in a resealable plastic bag so they're easier on the blades.

4 bananas, peeled and sliced into 2-inch pieces

¼ cup unsweetened flaked coconut

¼ cup coconut milk

2 tablespoons almond butter

1. Freeze the bananas for at least an hour or overnight.
2. Add the bananas to a food processor or blender. Pulse a few times to break down.
3. Add the flaked coconut, coconut milk, and almond butter and process until smooth, 3 to 4 minutes. Scrape down the sides of the food processor and serve immediately in chilled bowls or freeze for later enjoyment.

> **STORAGE:** Store this ice cream in the freezer for up to 2 months in single-serve containers so they can be pulled out at a moment's notice. Let thaw slightly before serving.
>
> **VARIATIONS:** For a chocolate version, omit the flaked coconut, add ¼ cup raw cacao powder, and top with cacao nibs (optional).

PER SERVING: Calories 412; Total fat: 20g; Total carbs: 60g; Fiber: 9g; Sugar: 31g; Protein: 7g; Sodium: 10mg

Lemon Tart with Nut Crust and Raspberry Sauce

Prep time: 10 minutes | **Cook time:** 15 to 20 minutes |
Makes 12 small triangles (1 triangle per serving)

This refreshing, satisfying lemon tart will brighten your day. If you don't have a food processor, substitute 3 to 4 cups almond meal. You can also swap the macadamia nuts for other raw nuts such as hazelnuts and pecans or a mixture.

CRUST:

3 cups raw macadamia nuts

½ cup coconut oil, melted

¼ teaspoon ground cinnamon

FILLING:

4 large eggs, at room temperature

3 tablespoons grated lemon zest (from 3 to 4 lemons)

½ cup lemon juice (from about 4 lemons)

½ cup coconut oil

2 tablespoons maple syrup

1 teaspoon alcohol-free vanilla extract

SAUCE:

1 cup fresh raspberries

1 teaspoon water

1. Preheat the oven to 350°F.
2. To make the crust, into a food processor put the nuts, coconut oil, and cinnamon and pulse until slightly chunky but sticky and dough-like.
3. Into the bottom of a 9-inch round tart pan, pie plate, or springform pan, press the crust mixture. Bake until the crust is set and slightly golden, about 10 minutes. Remove it from the oven and let it cool.
4. To make the filling, in a medium bowl beat the eggs; set aside.
5. Into a small saucepan put the lemon zest and juice, coconut oil, maple syrup, and vanilla and whisk to combine. Heat over medium heat until warm.
6. Spoon a few tablespoons of the heated mixture into the eggs, whisking constantly to temper the eggs. Add the egg mixture to the saucepan, reduce the heat to medium-low, and cook until thickened, whisking constantly.

> **CONTINUED ON NEXT PAGE**

Lemon Tart with Nut Crust and Raspberry Sauce

> **CONTINUED**

7. Pour the lemon filling into the crust, spreading it with a rubber spatula or wooden spoon into an even layer. Refrigerate until firmly set (it shouldn't jiggle when you shake it), about 1 hour.

8. Meanwhile, make the sauce. In a saucepan, heat the raspberries and water over medium heat, whisking until smooth with some chunks. Heat until warmed through and slightly thickened.

9. To serve, cut the tart into quarters and then cut each quarter into three small triangles. Top with the raspberry sauce.

STORAGE: The tart will keep in the refrigerator for 5 days. Or, cut into slices and freeze individually on a sheet tray, then transfer to a resealable plastic bag and freeze for up to 2 months for a quick treat.

VARIATION: Skip the sauce and top with fresh raspberries or other berries or Coconut Whipped Cream (see page 125).

MAKE IT FASTER: For a quicker sauce, you can microwave the raspberries with a teaspoon of water on high and mash with a fork into a chunky sauce.

PER SERVING: Calories 438; Total fat: 45g; Total carbs: 9g; Fiber: 4g; Sugar: 4g; Protein: 5g; Sodium: 27mg

Dessert Parfait with Coconut Whipped Cream

Prep time: 5 minutes | **Serves** 2

This is a super easy recipe for whipped cream with all the satisfaction and none of the dairy. Just make sure the can of coconut milk is thoroughly chilled before use, and do not shake the can before or after refrigerating.

1 (14-ounce) can full-fat coconut milk, chilled

½ teaspoon alcohol-free vanilla extract

2 cups fresh berries (blueberries, strawberries, raspberries, blackberries, or a mixture)

2 tablespoons chopped fresh mint, for garnish (optional)

1. Open the can of coconut milk without shaking it and scoop out the thickened coconut cream from the top into a medium bowl, reserving the water for drinking or a smoothie. Add the vanilla and whisk until thickened.

2. To serve, divide half of the berries between two chilled beverage glasses. Top with about 2 inches of the cream. Add the remaining berries and top with the remaining cream. Garnish with the mint (if using) and serve.

> **STORAGE:** Extra whipped cream will keep in the refrigerator for up to two days.
>
> **MAKE IT FASTER:** Purchase premade coconut cream and follow the directions on the package.

PER SERVING: Calories 503; Total fat: 48g; Total carbs: 22g; Fiber: 7g; Sugar: 14g; Protein: 6g; Sodium: 31mg

Cacao-Nut Truffles

Prep time: 5 minutes | **Makes** about 16 truffles

This is my go-to recipe for a Pegan-friendly, not-too-sweet chocolate fix. You can reduce the honey or maple syrup in the recipe or omit the cacao powder for a quick snack. Note that these melt and get sticky after a few minutes when not stored in the refrigerator or freezer.

1½ cups raw almonds

½ cup creamy unsalted almond butter

¼ cup raw cacao powder

3 tablespoons coconut oil, melted

2 tablespoons raw honey or maple syrup

¼ teaspoon ground cinnamon

1. Place the nuts in a food processor and pulse until finely ground. Add the remaining ingredients and pulse until a smooth, sticky dough forms, 1 to 2 minutes.

2. Scoop out 1 heaping tablespoon of dough at a time to form 1½-inch balls, placing them on an aluminum foil– or parchment paper–lined baking sheet or plate so they don't touch. Refrigerate the truffles until firm, about 1 hour.

STORAGE: Store truffles in the refrigerator for up to 2 weeks, or freeze up to 3 months. When storing in the freezer, first transfer the truffles to a resealable plastic bag.

INGREDIENT TIP: You can find raw cacao powder (typically packaged in a resealable plastic pouch) at specialty grocery stores.

VARIATIONS: If you don't have a food processor, substitute the raw almonds with 1½ cups almond meal or 1 cup almond meal and ½ cup ground flaxseeds. You can add extra flavor by rolling the truffles in extra cacao powder, unsweetened flaked coconut, a mixture of ground cinnamon and chili powder, or finely chopped nuts before refrigerating them.

PER SERVING: Calories 148; Total fat: 12g; Total carbs: 7g; Fiber: 3g; Sugar: 3g; Protein: 5g; Sodium: 1mg

GLYCEMIC INDEX/ GLYCEMIC LOAD CHART

This is a list of Pegan-friendly foods and their glycemic index and load numbers (based on information from University of Sydney). A glycemic index of 55 or less is considered low, 56 to 69 is considered moderate, and 70 and above is considered high. A glycemic load of 10 or less is low, 11 to 19 is moderate, and 20 or more is high. Some doctors recommend that those with diabetes or prediabetes keep glycemic loads to 20 or less for any 3-hour period, but anyone wanting to follow a low-carb diet can use this method for weight loss and blood sugar stabilization.

FOOD	SERVING SIZE	GLYCEMIC INDEX	GLYCEMIC LOAD
VEGETABLES			
ASPARAGUS	1 cup cooked or raw	1.4	20
BEETS, COOKED	2–3 slices	64	3
BELL PEPPERS	1 cup cooked or raw	1.4	20
BROCCOLI	1 cup cooked or raw	20	1.4
BUTTERNUT SQUASH	⅓ cup boiled, mashed	51	3
CABBAGE	1 cup cooked or raw	1.4	20
CARROTS, BOILED	½ cup	49	1.5
CAULIFLOWER	1 cup cooked or raw	20	1.4
CELERY	1 cup cooked or raw	1.4	20

FOOD	SERVING SIZE	GLYCEMIC INDEX	GLYCEMIC LOAD
COLLARD GREENS	1 cup cooked	20	1.4
EGGPLANT	1 cup cooked	1.4	20
GREEN BEANS	1 cup cooked or raw	1.4	20
KALE	1 cup cooked or 2 cups raw	1.4	20
LETTUCE	2 cups raw	20	1.4
MUSHROOMS	1 cup cooked or raw	1.4	20
PEAS, GREEN, BOILED	½ cup	48	2
PUMPKIN, BOILED	½ cup	75	4.5
SPINACH	1 cup cooked or 2 cups raw	20	1.4
SWEET POTATO (BAKED, SKIN ON)	5.3 ounces	94	42
SWISS CHARD	1 cup cooked	20	1.4
TOMATOES	1 cup cooked or raw	20	1.4
ZUCCHINI	1 cup cooked	1.4	20
FRUIT			
APPLE	4.25 ounces	38	9.6
BANANA	4.25 ounces	58	13
BLACKBERRY	4.25 ounces	54	5
BLUEBERRY	4.25 ounces	54	5
DATE (MEDJOOL)	2 ounces	36	18

FOOD	SERVING SIZE	GLYCEMIC INDEX	GLYCEMIC LOAD
GRAPEFRUIT	4.25 ounces	25	2.7
KIWI	4.25 ounces	52	7
LEMON	4.25 ounces	25	3
LIME	4.25 ounces	24	1
ORANGE	5.25 ounces	42	5.9
PINEAPPLE	4.25 ounces	51	6.6
RASPBERRY	4.25 ounces	54	5
STRAWBERRY	4.25 ounces	41	1
WATERMELON	5.25 ounces	72	7.6
LEGUMES			
CHICKPEAS, BOILED	5.25 ounces	28	8.4
LENTILS, COOKED	5.25 ounces	29	5.2

THE DIRTY DOZEN AND THE CLEAN FIFTEEN™

A nonprofit environmental watchdog organization called Environmental Working Group (EWG) looks at data supplied by the US Department of Agriculture (USDA) and the Food and Drug Administration (FDA) about pesticide residues. Each year it compiles a list of the best and worst pesticide loads found in commercial crops. You can use these lists to decide which fruits and vegetables to buy organic to minimize your exposure to pesticides and which produce is considered safe enough to buy conventionally. This does not mean they are pesticide-free, though, so wash these fruits and vegetables thoroughly. The list is updated annually, and you can find it online at EWG.org/FoodNews.

DIRTY DOZEN™

1. strawberries
2. spinach
3. kale
4. nectarines
5. apples
6. grapes
7. peaches
8. cherries
9. pears
10. tomatoes
11. celery
12. potatoes

†Additionally, nearly three-quarters of hot pepper samples contained pesticide residues.

CLEAN FIFTEEN™

1. avocados
2. sweet corn
3. pineapples
4. sweet peas (frozen)
5. onions
6. papayas
7. eggplants
8. asparagus
9. kiwis
10. cabbages
11. cauliflower
12. cantaloupes
13. broccoli
14. mushrooms
15. honeydew melons

MEASUREMENT CONVERSIONS

VOLUME EQUIVALENTS (LIQUID)

US STANDARD	US STANDARD (OUNCES)	METRIC (APPROXIMATE)
2 tablespoons	1 fl. oz.	30 mL
¼ cup	2 fl. oz.	60 mL
½ cup	4 fl. oz.	120 mL
1 cup	8 fl. oz.	240 mL
1½ cups	12 fl. oz.	355 mL
2 cups or 1 pint	16 fl. oz.	475 mL
4 cups or 1 quart	32 fl. oz.	1 L
1 gallon	128 fl. oz.	4 L

OVEN TEMPERATURES

FAHRENHEIT	CELSIUS (APPROXIMATE)
250°F	120°C
300°F	150°C
325°F	165°C
350°F	180°C
375°F	190°C
400°F	200°C
425°F	220°C
450°F	230°C

VOLUME EQUIVALENTS (DRY)

US STANDARD	METRIC (APPROXIMATE)
⅛ teaspoon	0.5 mL
¼ teaspoon	1 mL
½ teaspoon	2 mL
¾ teaspoon	4 mL
1 teaspoon	5 mL
1 tablespoon	15 mL
¼ cup	59 mL
⅓ cup	79 mL
½ cup	118 mL
⅔ cup	156 mL
¾ cup	177 mL
1 cup	235 mL
2 cups or 1 pint	475 mL
3 cups	700 mL
4 cups or 1 quart	1 L

WEIGHT EQUIVALENTS

US STANDARD	METRIC (APPROXIMATE)
½ ounce	15 g
1 ounce	30 g
2 ounces	60 g
4 ounces	115 g
8 ounces	225 g
12 ounces	340 g
16 ounces or 1 pound	455 g

RESOURCES

BOOKS

De Souza, R. J., A. Mente, A. Maroleanu, A. I. Cozma, V. Ha, et al., "Intake of Saturated and Trans Unsaturated Fatty Acids and Risk of All Cause Mortality, Cardiovascular Disease, and Type 2 Diabetes: Systematic Review and Meta-analysis of Observational Studies." *BMJ*. August 11, 2015. doi: 10.1136/bmj.h3978.

Hyman, Mark, MD. *The Blood Sugar Solution 10-Day Detox Diet*. New York: Little, Brown and Company, 2014.

——. *The Blood Sugar Solution: The UltraHealthy Program for Losing Weight, Preventing Disease, and Feeling Great Now!* New York: Little, Brown and Company, 2012.

——. *Eat Fat, Get Thin: Why the Fat We Eat Is the Key to Sustained Weight Loss and Vibrant Health*. New York: Little, Brown Spark, 2016.

——. *Food: What The Heck Should I Eat?* New York: Little, Brown Spark, 2018.

Levin, Amelia. *Paleo for Every Day: 4 Weeks of Paleo Diet Recipes & Meal Plans to Lose Weight & Improve Health*. Emeryville, CA: Rockridge Press, 2014.

Mente, A., L. de Koning, H. S. Shannon, and S. S. Anand. "A Systematic Review of the Evidence Supporting a Causal Link between Dietary Factors and Coronary Heart Disease." *Archives of Internal Medicine*. April 13, 2009. doi: 10.1001/.archinternmed.2009.38.

Spritzler, Franziska. "6 Foods That Cause Inflammation." *Healthline*. December 17, 2018. https://www.healthline.com/nutrition/6-foods-that-cause-inflammation.

WEBSITES

Consumer's Guide to Food Labels
AWIOnline.org/content/consumers-guide-food-labels-and-animal-welfare

Culinary Medicine
Feinberg.Northwestern.edu/sites/ocim/education/medical-students/culinary-medicine
-course.html

Dr. Andrew Weil
DrWeil.com

Dr. Oz
DoctorOz.com

Paleo Diet
MayoClinic.org/healthy-lifestyle/nutrition-and-healthy-eating/in-depth/paleo-diet/art-20111182

The Daniel Plan
DanielPlan.com/starthere

The University of Sydney's Glycemic Index
GlycemicIndex.com

US Department of Agriculture's Food Safety and Inspection Service's meat and poultry
labeling terms
www.FSIS.USDA.gov/wps/portal/fsis/topics/food-safety-education/get-answers/food-safety-fact
-sheets/food-labeling/meat-and-poultry-labeling-terms/meat-and-poultry-labeling-terms

Whole 30
Whole30.com/whole30-program-rules

ORGANIZATIONS

Animal Welfare Institute

AWIOnline.org

Monterey Bay Aquarium's Seafood Watch list

SeafoodWatch.org

Natural Resources Defense Council (NRDC)

NRDC.org

COMMODITY BOARDS

California Walnuts

Walnuts.org

National Honey Board

Honey.com

American Egg Board

IncredibleEgg.org

INDEX

ABOUT THE AUTHOR

AMELIA LEVIN is an award-winning cookbook author, food industry writer, certified chef, recipe developer, and former news reporter and magazine editor. She is the author of *Paleo for Every Day*, a Rockridge Press book, among other cookbooks, and contributes regularly to a variety of food and restaurant industry magazines. When she's not typing away on her computer or testing recipes and making Pegan-friendly meals in her kitchen, she enjoys working out, spending time with her family, and studying for a professional certification in holistic nutrition. She lives in Chicago with her husband (and primo taste-tester), Harvey Henao, and two children (taste-testers-in-training), Jonah and Liliana (Lily).

CPSIA information can be obtained
at www.ICGtesting.com
Printed in the USA
LVHW050554151019
633812LV00003BA/3/P

9 781641 526784